BEYOND THE BEDROOM

Healing for Adult Children
of Sex Addicts

Douglas Weiss, Ph.D.
Author of
Intimacy and *The Final Freedom*

Health Communications, Inc.
Deerfield Beach, Florida

www.hcibooks.com

Library of Congress Cataloging-in-Publication Data
is available from the Library of Congress

©2005 Douglas Weiss, Ph.D.
ISBN 0-7573-0325-0

Publisher: Health Communications, Inc.
            3201 S.W. 15th Street
            Deerfield Beach, FL 33442-8190

Cover design by Andrea Perrine Brower
Inside book design by Dawn Von Strolley Grove

Contents

The information in this book, including much of the direction and guidance, is taken from a comprehensive survey of male and female adult children of sex addicts (ACOSAs) conducted in the fall of 2004. The substance of the book is also based on my almost twenty years of professional experience helping to heal sex addicts and their families, as well as my personal experience as a recovering sex addict and adult child of sex addicts.

INTRODUCTION

My Story

Hi, my name is Doug, and I am an adult child of a sex addict. Here is what happened, what I have learned and where I am (gladly) today. My hope is that as you read about my strength, hope and experience, you will understand that it is not where you come from but only where you arrive that is critical. It is not the good or bad of what was given to you, but what you decided to make out of it that counts.

My mother, who was married with no children at age twenty, decided to act out sexually with another man. Her ongoing adultery with this other man brought about my conception. My mother's first husband divorced her when he discovered her behavior. The man who impregnated her abandoned her as well because he had impregnated someone else. He never showed up in my life, ever. So here she was, divorced, pregnant and abandoned. She became sexually involved with another man. She married this man, and he became my legal father. His name was Bill Weiss.

Bill was an alcoholic and also had other significant mental issues. They managed to stay together long enough to have three daughters. They divorced while my mother was pregnant with the last daughter.

My mother became a single mom, with four children to care for and feed, two still in diapers. Feeling overwhelmed, I'm sure, she tried to care for the family, but eventually we were all placed into separate foster homes. I was hustled from home to home to home due to my mother's complaints about each place. My first memory takes place in one of these foster homes. I remember that I was being noisy in a church and got a beating with a belt for this behavior. It's sad, I think, that my first memory did not involve my sexually addicted mother. Sadly, my heart never really attached to her because I was moved from place to place.

My mother, who was now without any children (she gave the baby up for adoption), was free to get a job and continue acting out with other men. Her favorite place to go was a bar to find men. She eventually found a man, and they moved in together. She was soon able to get a social worker to return her children to her.

Here, for the first time, I remember my sisters Debbie and Suzie. Her boyfriend at the time was Bob, and they were living together. It was shortly after this I remember starting first grade. There was a lot of chaos, rejection and inability to put the pieces together. This somehow was my life. Changing people, changing rules, changed systems, and now I was supposedly home. I learned to adapt to the world around me. I learned the language and who controlled the system, and I did the best I could to survive.

Bob and my mother eventually married. They just took off for about two days and left their children home alone. They had gone to Virginia to get married. As an adult, I can't imagine leaving three children for two days without any information. Then they came back and told us the "good news." It was bizarre, but we adaptive children just did what we did best—we adapted.

I was aware that my mother and Bob had pornography hidden in their bureaus. My parents verbalized sexual humor that at times was inappropriate. As time went on, my mom thought I needed to know about sex. When I was, somewhere between twelve and thirteen years old, she gave me a very thick book on sex. This book was sort of like a college textbook. I really don't remember much of what I read, but the pictures in the book became the platform that initiated and maintained my own future sexual addiction. This became an almost daily medication for me that temporarily eliminated the past pain and desire to somehow connect.

Sometime later, I remember walking across town. About five miles one way, a man asked if I wanted a ride. He gave me a lot of alcohol and then abused me. This was my first sexual encounter, and I was treated as an object. Shocked, I suppressed it and then adapted as usual.

I started to become sexually active in high school and quickly became out of control. The use of alcohol and drugs was a regular occurrence. Girlfriends and one-night stands were very common. I would go to bars where I thought I was picking up women. Most of these women were in their twenties or older, and I was under eighteen. It wasn't until later that I realized I was the one being picked up by adult female sex addicts who were using me as an object for sex. By the time I was in high school, I was already living with a twenty-three-year-old sexually addicted model. How insane!

My mom really didn't say much about it. I have to believe that at times she knew I was drunk, high or had girls in my room. This was all a reaction to being an adult child of a sexual addict. My mom really couldn't nurture her children. I'm sure she had her own guilt and shame to deal with. She sat in front of the television and zoned out for most of our evening hours if she wasn't working.

I definitely didn't learn how to be emotionally authentic. Emotions, if shared, were used later to shame and humiliate. Spirituality was not discussed, although we were dropped off on Sundays to go to the Salvation Army for a few years.

I definitely learned how to live with secrets: my secrets, my mother's secrets and extended family secrets. Duplicity in life was normal; it was always, "Do as I say, not as I do."

Feeling out of the norm was commonplace. I remember feeling so ashamed over my welfare token for lunch at school. I was emotionally, morally and spiritually underdeveloped.

I remember distinctly in high school projecting a false self that I had it together. I was as well dressed as I could be, confident and in shape on the outside. I was this falsely projected self well into my twenties. I did not have a clue how to be me. Materialism and partying were all I knew as a result of growing up as an adult child of a sex addict (ACOSA). I couldn't let people into my heart, even if it was to save my life. I had some really good-hearted women try to get close to me, but I couldn't go there. I definitely had the core belief that if you knew me, you wouldn't love me.

I would give myself away to people and be hurt. I had so many female sex addicts for girlfriends. They were beautiful, sexual and emotionally unavailable, and they would use me like an object and reject me. I had "good girl" relationships, too, but I really didn't feel good enough for them, so I would end them eventually.

When I was nineteen years old, I had a significant spiritual awakening, and alcohol and drugs stopped instantly in my life. But the brokenness of abuse, abandonment, shame and my sexual addiction all stayed. Finally, as I grew spiritually, layer after layer of dysfunction began to peel away.

When I married at twenty-three years of age, I was still damaged goods. Fortunately, I married a good girl—a really good girl. Lisa was beautiful and full of love and wisdom, which my soul desperately needed. My sexual addictions were already significantly in remission. Months into our marriage, I became totally sober and free of sexual addiction and have remained so for over eighteen years (no porn, self-behavior or behaviors with others). I have been able to stay monogamous with Lisa.

My false self took a while to heal, to get away from having to be always right and perfect. I worked in a treatment center after we married as a chemical dependency tech while working on two master's degrees.

I went to many Alcoholics Anonymous and Narcotics Anonymous meetings as part of my job. I was introduced to the Twelve Steps and started another layer of healing. I was able, over time, to give up my caffeine and sugar addictions and become the real me. I wasn't plastic or religious, but authentic and spiritual.

I was able to grapple with many of the issues that resulted from being the son of two sex addicts. I was able to address the abandonment and rejection from a male sex addict who was so self-absorbed that a child of his held none of his interest.

I was able to address and heal from my mother's addiction to sex. Nobody wants his parent to be a sex addict, especially his mother. I was able to accept her reactions to her abuse and abandonment from her own father and mother.

I did my own anger work and eventually forgave my mother. I asked her to forgive me years ago. On my fortieth birthday, she was able finally to apologize to me. She was, however, already forgiven. Now we can talk on the phone, and she is very supportive of my life and my family.

I started my private practice with a local psychiatrist in Texas. My clients immediately became almost exclusively sex addicts. Back then nobody knew what to do with sex addicts. Sex addiction wasn't even a known term.

I still remember the first time I met Pat Carnes. I had my own book, *Women Who Love Sex Addicts,* and was more than two years sexually clean and sober. Our first book in 1993, *Women Who Love Sex Addicts,* was one of the first books for partners of sexual addicts. We were on *Donahue, The Sally Jesse Raphael Show* and many other national television and radio shows, as well as in newspaper articles. It was amazing how well this book was received so early in the stage of sexual addiction recovery knowledge.

Later I wrote *The Final Freedom: Pioneering Sexual Addiction Recovery.* This book came out the week of the Bill Clinton and Monica Lewinsky scandal. I was in high demand everywhere in the media. Oprah even did a show on sexual addiction with me as a guest. Lifetime, the women's network, did a movie about a man who went through treatment for sex addiction at my Heart to Heart Counseling Center. The movie was called *Sex, Lies and Obsession.* We continue to carry the torch for sexual addiction healing.

I remember talking to God one day in college. I was asking him why he let all this junk happen to me: "If you were going to use me, why not for a nice-home, nice-life type of story?" For years I would periodically bring this question back up for discussion.

Now the question I ask is different: "Out of all the people who were born into this kind of mess, why did you pick me to get better?" Today, life is great. I have an authentic relationship with God, my wife, children, friends, coworkers, neighbors and myself. I am flawed, but loved; I make mistakes and progress all in the same week. I have been free from addictions for a very long time.

Life is really good. I get to help others like me. I enjoy meeting people at all stages of their journey. I remember being in a meeting with other counselors who work alongside me. We started talking about the impact of sex addiction on adults and teens today. I asked them how many had parents who were sexually addicted. I was amazed at how many raised their hands. I knew then I was heading into another frontier with adult children of sexual addicts.

As I read over the research conducted for this book, I was amazed that sex addiction had such a large impact on both the sons and daughters of addicts. But you can heal, and just like I have, stop it from going any further down your family tree.

1

What Is a Sexual Addiction?

Once again I am sitting in a comfortable chair in a television studio. Along with me are the host, lights, camera and "action" from the floor director. The most frequently asked question is, "So, Dr. Doug, what really is sexual addiction anyway?" I'm sure you're probably also sitting in your comfortable chair right now with the same question popping into your mind.

A sex addict, much like an alcoholic or overeater, uses his or her drug of choice (sex) to avoid past or present pain and escape the realities of life. The sex addict uses sex in such a way that many of the following questions would be answered with a "yes."

The Sexual Addict Quiz

1. Have you engaged sexual behaviors that you wish you could stop?
2. Do you feel abnormally driven by your sexual drive?
3. Have you been in relationships just for sex?
4. Has masturbation been ongoing even after marriage?
5. Has pornography continued for you after a long-term, committed, sexual relationship?
6. Does your sexuality seem to be dragging down your personal potential?
7. Do you find that you spend a significant amount of time online viewing pornography or grooming others for sexual encounters?
8. Have you experienced an unwanted sexual encounter during childhood or adolescence?
9. Has monogamous sex grown boring?

The sexual addict tends to have a secret sexual life. He or she has a normal exterior life as a citizen and parent, and may be politically, socially or spiritually active in the community. But he or she has a secret life of cruising, masturbating, and frequenting adult bookstores, Internet chat rooms or prostitutes, or having affairs.

Everything may look normal on the outside, but the addict suffers silently. Unable to be honest, the addict is unable to sustain a true, emotionally intimate relationship. He or she lives with a voice inside that says, *If you really knew me, you wouldn't love me.*

Personally and professionally I know the hell of this addiction, and it's not fun. Fortunately, there is now help. Unfortunately for most of you reading these pages, there may not have been help or information available on sexual addiction when your parents were in the midst of their struggles. Most suffered secretly with an addiction for which they hated themselves.

Now to make it more complicated, sex addiction is not limited to one behavior. A sex addict, whether male or female, can be addicted to a variety of sexual behaviors. Some of these behaviors are listed below, but problems are not limited to these:

- —Voyeurism
- —Pornography
- —Chat rooms
- —Sexual literature
- —Prostitutes
- —Masturbation
- —Cross-dressing
- —Fantasy
- —Fetishes
- —Exposing oneself
- —Affairs
- —One-night stands
- —Anonymous encounters

Some sex addicts have affairs outside of their marriage; some use their spouse in a sexually disconnected manner; some leave their spouse alone sexually, preferring masturbation, fantasy or pornography. A sexual addict is similar to an alcoholic, where some prefer martinis, scotch and water, or beer, but all alcoholics still use alcohol in a way that is destructive to their lives.

There are common characteristics of sexual addiction that are shared by all types of addicts. Sexual addicts are either in denial or rationalize why they do what they do. Similar to other addicts, they blame others for their addiction.

Several roads may have been taken to becoming sexually addicted. Many sexual addicts have been victims of sexual, emotional or physical abuse. Others got on the path of sexual addiction due to a reward system they set up with pornography and fantasy. Others have chemical imbalances and as adolescents they treated this with orgasm responses to feel better. If you want more detailed information on the origins of sexual addiction, I recommend my book *The Final Freedom: Pioneering Sexual Addiction Recovery.*

Sexual addiction is often confused with a high libido—another question I get asked frequently by the media. A man or woman with a high libido can have spirit, soul and body sex. He or she can also experience sexual satiation regularly. A high libido person enjoys relational sex—the key word here being "enjoys."

A sexual addict rarely if ever has sex in a spirit, soul and body manner. The sex addict often disconnects from his/her spouse during sexuality and orgasm. The sexual addict rarely feels satiated or satisfied sexually.

I think by now you can see why sexual addicts' lives might be chaotic and frustrating. They chase a high that can never satisfy them. They keep going for more, but they still aren't satisfied. They go for "different" (whatever that may mean to them), and that doesn't satisfy. They go to their endless fantasy world, and that doesn't satisfy. So they go to the Internet, and they are left disconnected once again.

Being a sex addict isn't fun. You feel alone, disconnected and often disqualified from the very best of life. A hug from a loving child is chilled by the memory of where you were that day. The "I love you" from your spouse seems shallow because of your secret life. Being unable to connect with those you love is the life of the sexual addict. Unfortunately, that means the sexual addict is not the only one impacted by his or her addiction.

Sexual addiction also has a huge impact on the spouse of a sexual addict. In our survey of adult children of sexual addicts, we found that most of the spouses were women and the sex addicts were men. Thus, if you are an adult child of a sexual addict, most likely your mother was the spouse of a sexual addict. It's also possible your mother was the sexual addict, which we will discuss shortly.

If your mother was the partner of a sex addict, the sex addiction probably had a tremendous impact on her soul. Who she was as a wife, friend, sexual partner, spiritual being and mother were all impacted. Her spouse was probably emotionally, spiritually and morally still an adolescent. He was also most likely extremely self-centered and insensitive to her needs. Her need for connection would have been unmet.

If she knew about her husband's addiction, her own sexuality could have been impacted or shamed. She probably felt like she never measured up and was married to a man for whom she was not his first love (the sex addiction was). There was also a 29 percent chance that her husband was a sexual anorexic.

As a sexual anorexic, her husband would have avoided her spiritually, emotionally and sexually. She may have gone months or years without sexual intimacy as he would use porn, masturbation, or have sexual or emotional relationships with others instead.

Sexual addiction in your family of origin may have resulted in the divorce of your parents. This divorce may also have brought into your life many individuals who your parents may have dated, married or even divorced.

I have worked with wives of sexual addicts for more than eighteen years. I can tell you in my professional experience that as a woman and a mother she is hurt, angry and impacted in almost every area of her life by this addiction. She alone often carries the secret of her husband's addiction.

In my book, *Partners: Healing from His Addiction,* I surveyed seventy wives of sexual addicts. The research shows that your mother had a large probability of struggling with depression, lower self-esteem and food issues. She may have acted out sexually herself, or alternatively became cold and distant to your suffering, or too clingy and manipulative.

I say all this so you can see that your mother and her parenting were impacted by the sexual addiction in your home. The mother she could have been and the mother you actually had were significantly different due to sex addiction.

A mother whose spiritual and emotional needs were being met would have been very different. A mother married to a man who truly was morally developed would have been different. A mother married to a man who wasn't self-absorbed and deceptive would have been different. A mother without the deep sense of betrayal from adultery or pornography would have been different. Without the secrets and the shame of your father's sexual addiction, your mother would have been different—and better.

Your mother had choices to make, but she also had fears of raising you alone, not feeling like she could work to make enough money and many others. She had reasons for her choices. Some of her reasons may have been less healthy than others, yet she was reacting to an unhealthy situation. If you grew up in a home with sexual addiction, then both parents were impacted. If your mother was a sexual addict, this would also have been true.

I think you're getting the picture that growing up in a family where there is a sexual addiction impacts all the family members. There still is one other person the sexual addiction would have impacted. That is *you*.

You have been impacted by the secret of sexual addiction. You had to react, adjust and grow up in an environment that sexual addiction was destroying. You didn't ask for this, and neither did I. But we can acknowledge the impact that sexual addiction has had on our lives.

We also have the choice to heal. We can stay unhealthy, or we can choose a lifestyle of recovery. I chose healing and recovery. My wife and children have had a man in their lives who did his own work to heal. My family is worth it, and I am worth healing.

You are worth it as well. The pages ahead will be insightful, and at times painful, but will definitely give you the possibility to place your feet on a path of tremendous healing. So grab hold of my hand and heart, and the hands and hearts of those who have participated in our survey, and we will walk together to a place called recovery.

Ashley's Story

My dad was an alcoholic and a sex addict/sexual anorexic. My mother struggled with borderline personality disorder and violent rages. Life was a daily hell-in-a-handbasket. We never knew what the evening was going to be like from one day to the next. One day we were hiding under the bed scared to death; the next day all was fine and dandy. My mother was in such turmoil all the time—she hated my dad. She hated him looking like the nice guy, while she was always seen as the crazy one.

I would stand outside my mother's door at night as a child and listen for noises to tell me if she was alive. I was convinced she would commit suicide, but if I could hear her crying at least I knew she was alive. My dad would be gone. He was either out drinking and "sexing," or downstairs reading. He was never available for us.

I started to notice early on that my mom was starving, and I couldn't figure it out. My dad seemed so nice and easy to be around. As I got older, I began to see that they never interacted with each other, so I began requesting that they talk or hold hands or kiss. It seemed odd, and I assumed a role that turned out to run my life later. The role was that of caretaker/facilitator—getting them to work it out was my mission.

They came to me for advice, and I would usually have some good advice for them. I tried to get them into therapy, but they never seemed to be on the same page when it came to "wanting help." As I took on this role, it interfered with everything: schoolwork, friends and boys. Everything normal got tainted by what was happening to my parents and to us kids.

I noticed all kinds of weird characteristics in my life that I didn't have control over, so I began attending Adult Children of Alcoholics (ACOA) meetings and that helped a lot; at least I could see other kids were suffering, too. I began to understand that my parents had a lot of addictions and that I was a product of that environment. I began to understand that I had built a lifestyle around helping them instead of centering my life around God. This was starving me of God's plan for my life.

I had so much confusion and rage, but I was determined to find my life. I read every book I could get my hands on, and learned and grew in my understanding of addiction and codependency. It was a hard road, but it felt good to be me.

Nine years ago my father died of cancer, and it was eye-opening because my mother changed. All of a sudden this woman I had known for thirty-one years was coming alive—she lost weight, she joined a gym, she took classes, she began to travel, and she started to spend money more freely. It was remarkable! And she would say over and over again, "I'm free to live now! I feel like all the hate just drained out of my body when your dad died." I can now see my mother, and it was incredibly healing and freeing for me to see her happy. It was freeing to break the silence in my household. We began to talk about it and deal with it.

Two years ago, I watched a video by Dr. Weiss called *Sexual Anorexia*. What happened to me as a child had a name—sexual anorexia. The slow, silent starving of our family through my father's addiction had a name! I shared this information with my brothers and with everyone I came across who had similar circumstances. I felt further freedom in my life to move out of the trap of addiction and into a life of peace. I see life as a journey, and I am learning every day how to walk free—and now I have the knowledge and tools to grasp what is happening and resolve it. I live with a loving husband and two children who love God, and I am involved in an exciting ministry where I use the gifts God gave me. There is life after being a child of a sex addict!

George's Story

I remember racing on my pride and joy, a Honda 50cc motorcycle, and hitting the roads outside the city limits in our rural agricultural community. I was off to visit an older woman in her mid-twenties. She was a friend who had pursued me. In my imagination I made it seem that she was my girlfriend. Nothing like this had happened to me before, and it seemed to awaken within me passions that I had no awareness of before that summer. I would often drive out to her home in the country. I would spend summer days with her in the family swimming pool, hang with her for a few hours, and then head back to my house in our small Midwestern community. It was the summer of my fourteenth year. The world was mine. You see, I had a crush on this woman. She unquestionably had my heart. She could make me feel alive, like nothing else I had ever encountered.

The interesting thing is that she had also captured my father's heart. He also was spending unusual amounts of time with her. In fact, one time when I was visiting this woman, my father, according to her, had also visited with her on that same day. She revealed that my father called her often. It wasn't long before I realized that my father was having an affair with this woman.

She became part of the bigger story in my father's life. This woman helped him redecorate our family home when my father sent my mother to another state to visit her sister. This woman picked out the carpet, helped paint, hung wallpaper; her personality was permanently fingerprinted in our home. My mother came back from her visit, walked into the house, and as I watched her face in horror I realized that she had been duped. My father somehow made this all seem plausible. He pulled off these types of things from time to time during the course of my parents' marriage.

My mother told her sons on several occasions that she was not my father's first choice for a marriage partner. Although they had dated, he actually pined for someone else and apparently settled for my mom. She grieved this, being an unloved married woman. Even to this day, now years after my father's death, the story is not far from my mother's heart.

My father was raised in a single-parent home. His father died when he was two years of age. My grandmother did not marry again. Although my father was not very open about his childhood, it appears he had a reckless upbringing. I have attempted to piece things together as best as I can. My father was different from his mother. She was extremely conservative, while he lived life as wildly as he could within the constraints of a religiously controlling environment.

As far back as I can recall, my father did not cherish or pursue my mother's heart. I can remember so many times on vacation, we would be walking in amusement parks or beaches or wherever, and my father and my older brother would be walking ten or fifteen paces ahead of my mother. I felt a responsibility not to let her be left behind so I would walk with her. I longed to be up with my dad, to be setting the pace. Over time I began to pity my mother. Even at quite a young age, I realized that my dad did not do anything purposefully to make my mother feel special. The design of their marriage was reflected in my mother's countenance. She did not seem to be a happy woman.

By the time I was in elementary school, I noticed that my father was friendly with other men's wives. He had a tendency to be too friendly. We would go out to eat at a restaurant, and he would be flirtatious with our waitperson. Instead of being impressive to his sons, as if it was "a guy thing," we were deeply disturbed. It was one of those things we never talked about. We could see what this did to our mother; it broke her. Over the years, I watched my father being nice, too nice, to other women—and not very nice to my own mother. I did not know enough to put words to this issue, but I was noticing nonetheless.

Over time, my mother would make comments regarding my father's behavior. Her strategy to remain connected or to "feel" attached to my father was to accuse, to become embittered, and to become negative. Now as I look back, this family system was modeled for my brothers and me; our lives were affected by my father's addiction, which was all about relationships. The majority of the time, these relationships appeared to take the form of emotional girlfriends, but some of these did move into the realm of the physical. He used these relationships to medicate himself. I have learned that addictions can take a variety of forms. For my dad, it was emotional girlfriends. It seemed that wherever we lived, wherever we moved, whatever he did, he had a girlfriend. Even in the latter years of his life, he found ways to be attached to other women and not my mother. This was incredibly painful for her. She became a desperate woman.

I grew up in a home that embraced the masculine. I only have brothers, and the way my father treated my mother made me believe that women's thoughts and ideas were of little significance. When I first married, it became painfully apparent that I had few skills or little understanding of the ways that women think and make sense of their world. Ultimately, I chose a path similar to the one that had been so graphically modeled by my father. I too found my marriage more difficult than I had hoped. I felt unskilled and alone. The answer to my problem seemed familiar. The solution seemed obvious; I would remain emotionally unattached from my wife and make emotional attachments to other women. I also made a promise to myself that these relationships would never become physical, as if that made it acceptable. My addictive behavior, which took the form of medicating my pain by emotionally using women, exhausted me and my wife, and took the life out of our marriage. It was also incredibly selfish and unkind to others. Our lives were filled with doubt; my wife did not trust me, and our marriage was void of any type of healthy connection. I violated the covenant with my wife; I committed adultery. The cost of not dealing with the pain of my early years, of choosing to medicate the pain instead of working toward healing, of choosing to follow a familiar path, cost me more than I wanted to pay, took me places I eventually did not want to go, and kept me longer than I wanted to stay.

By the mercy of God, his healing power in our lives and some close friends, I am grateful to say my life and marriage have been restored. The path God led me on was long. It was hard, lonely and often discouraging—and yet remarkably right. His path of recovery, his restoration has brought life.

Jessica's Story

Hi, my name is Jessica. I am thirty-one now. I was fifteen years old when my dad left our family. At first he told us that things were just "not working" with my mom. A few months later, we learned that he had been having extramarital affairs for the last five years. More and more lies were uncovered as time passed. I was shocked and horrified. On the surface we were a model family. Later I realized that was a front, behind which there was very little communication and a consistent avoidance of conflict.

There was an emphasis on social skill, status and external beauty. My father was fed by the attention and affirmation of other women. He lost his mother at the age of twelve and had to grow up really fast to help raise his six siblings. The absence of her in his life created a void, leading to what I now understand as sexual addiction in my father's life.

His behavior seemed to deteriorate even more after he moved out. He drank more and was in a number of relationships with women, one of which led to a marriage lasting just six months. I always hoped for the reconciliation of my parents. Unfortunately, his behavior drove their relationship to its end.

As a result of the breakdown of my family, the things I thought would be constant in my life experience had fallen apart. My own father had threatened to exit our lives altogether with a move to another state if we would not accept his current mistress. I was accommodating to save myself from further loss. What a mess!

The tendency for me to please people and live in a performance-oriented fashion was hard to quit. I felt as though I would be abandoned if I did not meet another person's expectations. If my own father left us, what would keep anyone else from leaving me? Relationships were very objectified—they served a purpose rather than yielding true connection and intimacy.

In telling my story, I must include that a few years later my older sister and I connected with God and became Christians. This was very helpful as it grounded me and began the healing of my heart. Looking back, I can see ways my father's issues bled through in the rest of our lives before there was an obvious problem. I remember my father commenting on my appearance regularly. This was especially uncomfortable during puberty and devastating when the comments were made in the presence of others. He would also remark about the state of other people . . . weight gained, weight lost, wealth, and the accumulation or loss of things.

I remember him flirting with other women. I remember times when he was tipsy and he would "inadvertently" touch my rear. I remember my relationship with Dad not really being relational because it was more important that he be productive.

For instance, any conversation with my father during a ride up a chairlift would be competing with *Time* magazine, sips of peppermint schnapps and classical music blaring through his headphones. Dinner was consumed while watching *Jeopardy,* and afternoons were spent with basketball games on the TV while my dad read the newspaper and shined shoes: multitasking at its best, relationships at their worst. I was something else to check off on a list.

I recall times my mom and dad would be very tense but nothing was processed: just a lot of clear messages beneath the surface, but rarely anything verbalized. I learned that art of behaving accordingly.

All this drastically affected my relationships with men and my view of them. I had the tendency to lose myself in what a man wanted me to be in order to get the security and acceptance I was so hungry for. I felt a conflicted desire: On one hand I wanted to reject them before they could reject me, but on the other I had an overwhelming need for their approval. My pattern was to continually date, but only for short periods of a few weeks or months. I was not promiscuous. The relationships involved kissing and some exploration. I was determined not to be used, but I did recognize the power of sexuality in a relationship.

I was aghast when early in high school my dad suggested that I get on the Pill (I had been dating a guy for just two weeks!). Now I can see it was a reflection of his promiscuous lifestyle being projected onto me. Though I was shocked at the time, his continuous offers led to my having premarital sex in a future relationship. I certainly carried the performance-oriented dynamic into my sexual life. I was supposed to be good at it and a source of pleasure, but my enjoyment really didn't matter. Sadly, it took a few years into my ten-year marriage for me to really experience the mutual satisfaction of a sexual relationship. What a difference.

Thankfully, there were a few great male leaders in my life who healed my warped perspective. One of them is my wonderful husband. He endured a lot of undeserved mistrust and held steady when I attempted to drive him away. The others were the pastors at my church. What a contrast to experience being valued unconditionally and to be taught life principles that they showed by example. I was very protective and resisted being vulnerable at first. It was so inviting, though—the freedom, the life and the healing. It was a process, but not an easy one. I had to rework a lot of patterns in my thinking, feelings and behavior. And a lot of the emotions I had worked so hard to shut down and avoid had to be let out, too. Parts of my heart were resurrected, and the lenses through which I viewed the world greatly transformed! It was very hard at first, and my inclination was to run from the pain rather than moving through it to healing. But as I took each step, I was more eager to take the next because of the level of freedom and wholeness that I began to experience. Also, the depth and richness to relationships just kept getting better.

2
_____

It's Time to Heal Again!

In the 1930s, American culture began to deal with alcohol as an
addiction. Alcoholics Anonymous was formed, and the Twelve
Step program was created. In the 1970s, we began to address
drug addiction. In the 1980s, the medical profession studied addictions to food and gambling. In the 1990s, there was the start of a
serious movement looking into sexual addiction and its recovery.
There is now an openness to address sexual addiction that we
haven't experienced before—and yet there are still misconceptions.
For example, it is interesting to me that a culture such as ours will

put almost any type of sexual behavior on television, but on the other hand will add a disclaimer warning "not for young audiences" on a show that talks straight about how to recover from sexual addiction. What a contradiction! (I actually experienced this as a guest on talk shows dealing with sexual addiction recovery.)

Looking beyond this contradiction, the medical and psychological communities are finally opening up to the reality of sexual addiction. Sexual addiction and other addictive behaviors have been observed for as long as recorded history. It took quite a while for people to move from seeing alcoholics as drunks who can't hold their liquor to people who have a treatable disease. Currently, it is almost in vogue to be recovering from "something," whether it is alcohol, drugs or shopping!

I believe we are in the early stages of understanding sex addiction in our culture. In the 1990s, in one television studio audience where I was a guest, only 25 percent of the people had heard of sex addiction. During the same year at a speaking engagement in a major university, I asked how many had heard of sex addiction. Again, I received a 25 percent show of hands. Today there's more awareness due to the print, television and radio attention given to sexual addiction. So I believe we are making progress in sex addiction awareness.

And it happened just in time because the Internet opened the floodgates for sexual addicts. The Internet not only provides pornography, chat rooms and sex cams, but it also provides e-mail pornography that anyone at any age can get. The Internet has a toxic lure of anonymity. Now men and women can act out literally for hours and days, and often nobody else knows. They don't even have to leave the house.

Not only is the Internet more anonymous, but it's more specific. Every fetish known to man or woman, legal or illegal, is depicted on the Internet on hundreds of millions of sex Web sites; anyone could be tempted. The sad thing is that in the twenty-first century, we provide these toxic images to our children. Sex addiction has not only become much more prevalent, but much more damaging to those who drink from the Internet.

Because I believe sex addiction transcends cultures, I want to broaden the concept of sex addiction beyond being merely an American phenomenon. There are sex addicts in every country. This is a worldwide problem. Fortunately, just like alcoholism, it can be treated, and people can be restored to sanity no matter what language they speak or in what culture they live. We live in an exciting time when people are seeking help for their addictions—and for the first time, help is available. We are finally coming to a place of healing again.

After the alcoholic movement, there was a large focus on the wife of the alcoholic. The whole codependency movement of the late 1970s and 1980s was born when professionals starting to look at the impact of alcoholism on the alcoholic's wife.

Then, finally, the alcohol movement, with all its wealthy treatment centers, was taken to a "heal again" state. Adult Children of Alcoholics (ACOA) was born out of the heart of Janet Woititz in her classic book *Adult Children of Alcoholics*. This book and others like it became its own movement.

Many in the alcoholic community, namely alcoholics and spouses of alcoholics, had to heal again. They already saw themselves as addicted or co-addicted, but now they were able to see themselves as ACOAs. Not all people raised in an alcoholic home are alcoholics or marry alcoholics, although some do. Woititz's book on adult children of alcoholics went way beyond the recovery community into the mainstream culture.

Adult Children of Alcoholics became a bestseller. It seemed that many more people were impacted by being raised in an alcoholic family than was previously known. The Twelve Step community began to adapt to this "healing again" and provided support groups for ACOAs.

Today, these groups are in almost every major city in the United States and around the world. This group of people was able to address the wounds that came from being around someone who was in pain and chose alcohol to medicate his or her pain.

In the sex addiction community, we are in the exact same place today as Janet Woititz was years ago. We first started with the sex addict treatment centers. Professionals were so focused on "him" getting better that they often didn't see the devastation of the wife.

At first clinicians made the mistake of calling all wives of sex addicts codependents. Then they started calling them partners of sex addicts. Finally, in the late 1990s, we started to look at female sex addicts and began to treat them and their spouses more intelligently.

Now we, as a recovering community, are at a "healing again" stage. We finally evaluated the impact of being raised in a home where one or both parents are sexually addicted. Now is the time when many of us will get a chance to heal again, and others will start a journey of insight and healing. Now we will, for the first time, really study this impact and start a path toward healing from being an adult child of a sexual addict.

There are many pioneers on this journey toward healing. As pioneers, we are the first to taste the fruit of recovery before the rest of the culture. In addition, we get to pave the way for others in how to deal with those who don't understand. As a pioneer, you may often be misunderstood by others who have not yet come to understand the plight of being an ACOSA.

Few have gone before us, but many will come after us. As a pioneer, you are the future leader of this movement. As you get some recovery behind you, and eventually years of recovery, you will gain experience and understanding of something that very few understand, including professionals. Many, I believe, who are starting their recovery today will be tomorrow's experts. The current misunderstandings of what you are doing will make sense to others years from now—and the journey will have been worth it for your sake and countless others.

I personally started my journey many years ago, and I am thankful that I did. I was healing from the wounds of being an ACOSA way before these letters were put together. I find it an honor to heal and then help others to heal, but only after I figured out some of these issues myself. I didn't know this was my future when I was working on my early recovery and was healing from past abuse, neglect and abandonment issues. These issues are a direct result of being an adult child of sexually addicted parents.

Was it worth it to be misunderstood and in pain? YES! Today I have the opportunity to see others heal from their ACOSA issues as they hear this message and respond to the healing process. Their choice to go on the journey makes my recovery, and the boundaries I must keep to maintain my healing, very worthwhile. One life like yours or mine can help many people begin and maintain recovery from the effects of our parent's sex addiction.

There is no shame in being a recovering ACOSA, just like there is no shame being a recovering anything. Of all the people who could have taken responsibility for their lives and behaviors, you have. I have no shame about being a recovering ACOSA. My father and mother didn't know they had the disease of sexual addiction, and neither did anyone else in my family. I am the first one who had a chance at recovering and helping to stop this disease from moving any further down my family tree. You may be the first in your entire lineage to acknowledge this disease. Recovering from the effects of being an ACOSA may be one of the largest contributions you will leave your future generations. I am proud of your efforts in considering this journey. There is more and more hope for you in each step you take.

3

Our Experiences

One of the greatest comforts in recovery, regardless of the type of addiction, is the fact that others have been where you are as well. Whether it be AA, NA, OA, SA or ACOSAs, we all have similar experiences. I remember in recovery literature someone said, "It's as if we grew up in the same family but hundreds of miles apart." This is definitely true of ACOSAs.

I want to expose you to some real people with real experiences. I do this because the power of the group is so strong. These real hearts express our experiences better than any I could hope to write.

In our survey, I asked ACOSAs from all over the world to answer some questions. Below are their responses about how they found out about their parents' sex addiction. I encourage you to read a section at a time and reflect. You might even have some feelings come up while reading these stories.

How I Found Out

I could hear the sounds from her bedroom. She would sleep with man after man. We would spend the night with one of her "friends," and while in my sleeping room, I could hear the sounds coming from the bedroom. If ever I suggested anything about this behavior, she would act as if nothing was wrong. To this day she would never admit that behavior. It is as if she was living another life back then.

—Rose

Initially, finding Playboys, *etc., under his bed. Later, he left Mom for another woman and then married her. Some years later, they separated because he had an affair. He has continued to have numerous sexual partners since. He fought in Vietnam and says he had sexual relationships there, including prostitutes.*

—David

I was around five years old and always remember sexual comments being made around me, seeing movies with sexual acts in them, and seeing pornography in large quantities in my parents' room, along with Playboys, Hustler *magazines and sex toys.*

—Fran

My father caught me looking at pornography on the Internet, and he started to tell me about his own problems with it.

—Tom

When I was twelve years old, my dad sent me out to his truck (parked in the driveway) to get his spare set of keys, which were hidden under the driver's seat. When I reached under the seat to get the keys, I found a pornographic magazine. Since I knew that porn was used to masturbate, finding the hard-core pornography revealed to me that my dad was most likely also masturbating. I knew that I would have to keep this discovery a secret and not tell my mom. So it became a secret of my dad's that I carried.

—Jean

When I realized my own sex addictions.

—Mike

I was looking through the computer at home and found some Internet cookies that looked like pornography sites. I thought it was my brother's Internet usage so I told my dad. He sat my brother and me down and told us everything about his addiction to pornography and masturbation. My dad was a pastor and so this totally burst my idealistic view of him. I went through a long time of soul searching after finding out about this.

—Jake

Only later as I received information about sexual addiction in my graduate school studies did I recognize that my stepfather had been a sexual addict. Looking back, I can see clear signs of this. I wish that he had been more careful not to leave those printed materials around where his children could find them. I received a very skewed and incomplete education about how to behave as a man.

—Rob

Now I want to expose you to some statistics relating to the age that our responders found out about their parent's sex addiction. I

was amazed at how young they were when they were made aware
of their parent's sexual addiction:

8% Before age 5	0% Ages 26–30
36% Ages 6–10	13% Ages 31–40
15% Ages 11–15	13% Ages 41–50
8% Ages 16–18	2% Ages 51 or above
5% Ages 19–25	

Most of us were too young to truly understand our parent's sex
addiction, but the secrecy and shame many of us felt had a great
impact on our development. Right now I want to share exactly how
we found out about our parents' sex addiction:

7.5% They confessed

11% They involved me in keeping a secret of their addiction

48% I found something that involved their addiction

7.5% My other parent told me

4% Another family member other than my parent told me

0% A person my parent acted out with sexually told me

22% Other

To go one step further, I asked ACOSAs about what behaviors
they became aware of by their sexually addicted parent. We had to
ask about Dad *and* Mom because some had a mother, or a mother
and father, who were sexually addicted.

If father was/is a sexual addict, which of the following behaviors
were you aware of:

20% Masturbation

39% Pornography

4% Affair one time

26% Multiple affairs

3% Homosexual behavior

8% Prostitutes

If mother was/is a sexual addict, which of the following behaviors were you aware of:

37% Masturbation
18% Pornography
18% Affair one time
27% Multiple affairs
 0% Homosexual behavior
 0% Prostitutes

You can see that many knew way too much information way too at a very early age. Sex addicts are usually in denial of how much their children, even very young children, know about their sex addiction. It is the classic saying, "The addict is the last to know."

Not only did ACOSAs have a secret to keep, but they also had some experiences about marriage they shared in our survey. We simply asked them to describe their parents' marriage. Here is what they had to say.

My parents have been married for fifty three years. They almost divorced, but they decided to stay together for the money. They are both very angry and abusive people. My mother believes she is helpless to leave him. My father is still a sex and food addict, and my mother is very codependent. I no longer have a relationship with my father. I see my mother infrequently.

—Jean

Cold, unfruitful, sad, trying, unloving.

—Brock

My stepfather has cheated on my mother many times since then, but Mom is dependent on him to the point that she will do anything he tells her to do. Including being with other men on one occasion.

—Carla

As far as I know my mother has never chastised my father for his sexual addiction. She has always been more concerned with his emotional and depression issues . . . which are probably symptoms of his sexual behavior.

—Tom

After twenty-five years of marriage, they still have frustrations with each other and can't seem to develop past a certain level of intimacy, but both are very patient and neither has talked about divorce, nor would they ever consider it from what I can see. They aren't very romantic, but they do live together fairly peacefully.

—Rick

Mom is codependent, highly sensitive; Dad does not show his feelings/emotions. They love each other a lot, but obviously did not have a truly honest marriage.

—Trent

It was hell . . . a lot of fighting and also a lot of neglect and abuse. They didn't really act like they cared much for us in those years. Honestly, my dad still doesn't act like he cares. My mom, though, seems to be genuinely repentant.

—Jackie

My stepfather and mother had a broken, distant relationship that died completely after his extramarital affair. They lived together until death but were never intimate.

—Rob

As you can see, most of us didn't grow up in a *Leave it to Beaver* home. There was only one respondent who felt his parents' marriage was healthy "but ignorant of the addiction."

This is meant to help you not feel alone or crazy. You experienced what you know to be true. For most of us there will be a degree of healing that will have to take place not only because of what we knew and when we knew about it, but also how we lived with it.

At the end of this chapter, I want you to see what some had to say about how they feel regarding having a sexually addicted parent. You may have had different experiences, but listen to this group and see if you can find something you didn't know that impacted you.

I held unhealthy attitudes toward women, looking at them for physical beauty only.

—Ken

My own husband has just completed a year of sobriety from pornography. I believe part of the reason I became involved in such a relationship in the first place was because of my father's addiction and how I viewed my own sexuality through this lens. I came to believe this was normal and to be expected. I believed a woman was for pleasure only, and needed to be good at "it" in order to retain her favor from a man. This was my only form of love.

—Brenda

I understood that my father needed to masturbate or have sex to visuals of other women to achieve orgasm. Therefore, I thought I MUST look like women in porn. I focused my life from fifth grade on to look as sexually beautiful as I could. I became image-obsessed/fashion-obsessed.

—Fran

I believe the way I perceive a normal relationship between father and daughter has been totally distorted, along with any natural relationship between a man and woman. I struggle with trust. Sex and

*the knowledge of it have been a part of my life as far back as I can
remember.*

—Amanda

*I believe I receive value from my sexuality, and that as a woman I
have no intrinsic value apart from being married. I believe women are
more valuable if they are attractive, and I was taught (by my Christian
father) that if a man doesn't get sexual gratification at home from his
wife, he is entitled to go outside of the marriage to get it.*

—Sandi

*I have struggled with trust, and I manage to hook up with men
with sexual addiction problems; my husband left me for another
woman. I am raising three boys and one girl on my own; it has been
hard to raise boys and understand things that are natural for boys,
and it scares me to death what could happen to them because of
another's sexual addiction.*

—Amanda

*Self-esteem issues, weight problems, ongoing addiction issues, no
clear role model, no real hope for the recovery process to work.*

—Jackie

*My father was a voyeur and incapable of healthy intimacy. His
rejection of me and his lure toward the visual took me into a world
where I became sexually addicted myself, and he watched me at
night while I masturbated. I would try to hide, but he was very
sneaky. He was also addicted to porn. As an adult, I have been
diagnosed with borderline personality disorder, sexual addiction and
food addiction. I struggle with codependency issues, and I feel
worthless and unlovable.*

—Jean

Contributed to my pornography addiction. Enabled my promiscuity. Affected my marriages. My view of God. Facilitated my turning myself in for molesting two teenage girls. My negative views of myself.

—Brian

Knowing such things about your parents is hard to take. Then, as an adult, I ran off into dark areas of sexuality. There I thought I was normal, and I was even proud of what I was doing. I didn't know for quite a while that I was not normal, nor was I proud anymore. I don't think either tangent has been good for me. I want to be responsible in all areas, especially in the sexual arena. I don't want to spend irresponsibly on "sexy" things that are not needed in a godly bedroom. I don't want to be a stressed-out mother lashing out at the kids because of the guilt that plagues me. I don't want to live under a cloud of depression for the sins of my parents or my own sins, when there is so much living to do. I pray a lot now.

—Jackie

By not being willing or able to label his behavior, I inadvertently ended up marrying someone with the same addiction—just packaged differently. I was not self-aware enough to realize what I needed in a mate and what kinds of behaviors he brought out in me that were exactly as I treated my dad. His addiction fueled my need to be perceived as responsible and a fixer. The tragedy is that it took being faced with my husband's secret addiction before I was able to face my father's addiction and my resulting codependent behaviors. I was sexually active way too early (fourteen) for all the wrong reasons— he told me he probably wouldn't date me anymore if I wasn't. Finally, I never had any kind of healthy sex information so I worked from my own thoughts and those of a bunch of other ill-informed teenagers.

—Alice

As you can see, many of us were in the same type of families but miles apart. As an ACOSA, you can heal so that your children's stories have a greater chance to be significantly different. It is work, but it is worth it for your children to have a much better chance at being healthy and loved adults.

This may be sensitive, yet we have to discuss our experiences of sexuality. No book on ACOSAs would be complete without discussing sexuality.

Our Sexuality

The impact on our sexuality as ACOSAs can be huge and decades long. Sex is the most powerful aspect of ourselves. Sexuality impacts our spirit, soul (mind, will and emotions), and our body. Our sexual health or lack of sexual health can impact our relationship choices, our sexual choices and our marriages.

Sexual Messages

Growing up in a home with a sexually addicted parent(s) is interesting. You receive all kinds of messages. The messages you get about sex can be very different from messages about sex in a healthy family.

We asked those who participated in our research survey about the messages they received from their parents. The first messages this group of ACOSAs share are messages from their father. The second group of messages is about sexual messages they received from their mother.

SEXUAL MESSAGES FROM DAD:

It was to be treated lightly, no need to be true to one woman.

—John

Being an attractive woman and marrying a successful man is the best a woman can achieve.

—Sandi

Looks are everything.

—Tonya

I was born to be used by men.

—Amanda

.

I was good for just one thing.

—Carla

Be beautiful, that's your worth; be responsive and willing.

—Brenda

"You are nothing if I am not drawn to you sexually" and "If I am drawn to you sexually, you are a slut."

—Jean

Don't do it. You don't want to be a hussy! We go to church and religious people don't do things like that.

—Jackie

SEXUAL MESSAGES FROM MOM

Sex is dirty, nasty, terrible. Sex is disgusting.

—Jean

Keep your mouth shut and remember the man is the head of the house.

—Carla

It is a natural thing. The human body is beautiful. Never be ashamed of who you are. You can talk to me about anything.

—Jackie

Sex was God's creation; I should enjoy it even to the detriment of other people, with whomever I could.

—John

It was something very secret and dirty. Not something good Christians discussed.

—Brian

Her attitude was, "It feels good, do it." If she couldn't find a man she liked or got bored with one, she would just move on to another one.

—Rose

Sex is awful, something to be suffered through.

—Brenda

Being godly and submissive is the best a woman can achieve.

—Sandi

Areas of Sexual Impact on ACOSAs

The impact of such messages on a child or adolescent would be devastating. Rarely does the ACOSA learn about abstinence before marriage, boundaries, sexual health, pregnancy or STDs. The bizarre, confusing and often conflicting messages about sexuality leave an ACOSA terribly vulnerable. You are vulnerable to believe what your adolescent peers are telling you about sex. You are also very prone to accept what pornography, your own sexual experiences or even what you have put together about your parent's experience have to tell you about sex. Regardless, this is an area in which few go unscathed as an adult child of a sexual addict.

The range of impact can be from sexual obsession to sexual avoidance. My clinical experience of ACOSAs is that there is a disconnect for them sexually. Rarely do they know how to have spirit, soul and body sex. The chapters on Sexual Wholeness and Intimacy Ever After will help the ACOSA achieve better levels of intimacy, including sexual intimacy.

Not only did we get mixed verbal messages from our parents, but many of us also had another interesting sexual occurrence. The largest percentage of us (67 percent) found out about our parent's sexual addiction during childhood or adolescence. In other words, the majority discovered their parent's sexual addiction during their own sexual development. What an impact this experience could have had on their sexuality!

Remember also how they found out about their parent's sexual addiction. Most of them (48 percent) found out about their parent's sexual addiction by finding something that involved their parent's addiction.

So the average ACOSA would have been between six and eighteen when they found out about their parent's addiction. They most likely found out by discovering pornography. They were aware at an early age about the pornography or affairs of their parent.

There is little doubt that these sexual experiences would impact our sexuality. In the following sections, I want to walk through three distinct areas of sexual impact you might have had or still are having issues with as an ACOSA.

Area One: Abuse

As a clinician, I know, in general, that one in three women and one in six men will be sexual abuse survivors. These studies usually define sexual abuse as a sex act with someone three or more years older than you. This is definitely abuse by most people's clinical or legal definitions if you are under the age of eighteen.

Although some ACOSAs experience sexual abuse by a parent, friend of the family, neighbor or stranger, many ACOSAs grow up with very unhealthy messages about sex that are also considered abusive to their sexual being.

A father or mother who sends the message that sex outside of marriage is acceptable can be seen as abusing a child's sexuality. A parent who exposes a child to pornography, prostitutes or other lovers is abusing the sexual soul of the child.

Many ACOSAs have sexual abuse issues that do not involve genital contact. The women who grew up thinking they were only good for sex have also experienced an abuse of their sexuality. The man who grows up being told to use women sexually has also had his innocent sexuality abused. As ACOSAs, we have to look at our nongenital sexuality as well as our genital sexuality to evaluate the sexual abuse to which our souls might have been exposed.

Area Two: Sexual Addiction

For many of us, our parent's addiction has also become our own. It's true that like alcoholism, workaholism and overeating, this addiction runs in families. Whether it is a disposition or environment or both, we do know clinically that sex addictions run in families.

For over seventeen years, I have heard men and women who were sex addicts tell of their parent's addictions. This doesn't mean we don't have choices or responsibility for our choices; it just means it is a variable to becoming a sexual addict.

A sex addict uses fantasy, lusting, grooming, pornography, the Internet, flirting, picking up people, sex acts of any variety or sexual behaviors to escape past pain or present life issues. He or she does these behaviors regardless of consequences they may have already had. They tend to have a secret sexual life that nobody knows about.

They tend to sexualize any appreciation or kindness toward them. They have tried to stop several times. They tend to believe at their core that if you really knew them, you wouldn't love them.

If you struggle with sexual addiction, you might be the very first in your lineage to have enough information to get better. If you are reading this book, you probably want to stop the addiction from going any further down your family tree.

You are worth being healed from sexual addiction. I have been free now for close to two decades. I know how to stay free and have taught thousands how to get and stay free from sexual addiction.

Area Three: Sexual Anorexia

This is another area of sexuality that may have impacted the ACOSA. The acting-out addict is easier to spot than the sexual anorexic. The sexual anorexic actively withholds spiritual, emotional and sexual intimacy. Not all sexual anorexics withhold sex, but many do.

Below I will give you nine statements. Assess these as you believe your spouse would assess them about you. Would your spouse agree or disagree with these statements?

1. My spouse keeps him or herself so busy that he/she has little time just for me.
2. When there are difficulties or conflicts in our marriage, my spouse focuses on me or blames me for them.
3. My spouse limits or withholds love from me.
4. My spouse limits or withholds praise from me.
5. My spouse limits or withholds sex from me.
6. My spouse has ongoing or ungrounded criticism of me.
7. My spouse uses anger or silence to control our relationship.
8. My spouse is unwilling or unable to share his or her feelings with me.
9. My spouse is controlling or shaming about money or financial issues.

If you think your spouse would have agreed with five or more of the previous statements, you may be sexually anorexic. Yes, you can be a sexual addict *and* a sexual anorexic. Approximately one-third of sex addicts are sexual anorexics as well.

The sexual anorexic "acts in." They withhold love, praise and connection. They won't give you their heart. If they are threatened with divorce, they will straighten up for a couple of weeks, but they slowly go back to that roommate approach to your marriage.

Sexual anorexia only shows up in marriage. Everyone else thinks the anorexic is a great person. It is only at home that the spouse and often family members are starved for connectedness. If this is ringing familiar to you, I highly recommend the video *Sexual Anorexia*. This will help you get started. Most sexual anorexics need professional help to attach to their spouses. I have seen couples who have not had sex or intimacy in ten years get better. So if you struggle in this area, be proactive.

❄ ❄ ❄

As ACOSAs we have many experiences and have been impacted sexually. We may have continued the bad messages about sex that we learned at home. We may have made our own bad sexual choices. We might have secrets, addictions, abuses or be sexually anorexic in our lives.

Regardless of the impact of our parent's sexual addiction on our lives, we are now responsible to heal and make ourselves whole. I encourage you to keep reading and apply what you can in order to heal your areas of hurt. It is your turn now to turn your experiences into strength and hope.

4

Our Development

M ost ACOSAs did not have a "normal" experience growing up. Most found out about their parent's sex addiction as children. For others it was during adolescence or
adulthood.

Regardless of whether you knew consciously about the addiction
in childhood, your development could still have been impacted. As
you look back, you may see holes or damage that may have
occurred. I asked those in our survey to share some of the negative
consequences they have experienced as a child, adolescent and adult.

As a child (0–12)

Self-esteem—negative comments from my father.

—Tonya

I don't know if it is specifically due to my father's addiction, but I found a pornographic magazine at age seven (at school) and was masturbating every night by age ten.

—Tom

A lack of concern for staying away from anything sexual as a child.

—Rick

I was exposed to pornography that was confusing. There was also alcohol, which was around way too much. Finally, they left me with an older boy as a babysitter who attempted to sexually molest me.

—Alice

My brother and some of his friends acted out with me when I was younger, I believe as a result of my father's addiction. I lost a two-parent family because of his affairs.

—Brenda

I lost the innocence of childhood. I was unable to keep friends due to my negative behaviors. I was not allowed to be in any groups related to school (Bluebirds, Brownies, cheerleading). I was not cared for emotionally or physically and was allowed to view pornography and stay home only, so I missed out on peer relationships.

—Fran

I was not able to play as a normal child. I had to be very hyper-vigilant, and I could not be spontaneous or make mistakes. I had to behave as an adult. The sex addiction in our family caused me to lose my innocence, and it took away my ability to trust and relate in healthy ways.

—Jean

Loss of self-respect, self-esteem and moral values. As a child, I thought her mother behavior was normal, but to some extent I knew that it wasn't. I desperately wanted to stand in her crowded room and scream, "This is wrong!!!" Her favorite sayings were, "Do as I say . . . not as I do" and "You're the child and I'm the parent."

—Rose

As an adolescent (13-19)

Sexual encounters, or even just touching was never an issue; I never realized I had a choice. Loss of innocence and choice—neither existed in my life.

—Tom

I was very obsessed with sex.

—Brian

I never felt close to my father. My mother would complain to me about how mean he was. I felt trapped in my loyalties.

—Ken

I was slowly led into darker and darker things, like pornography and the like. I knew these were wrong, but I didn't have the strength to stop them.

—Rick

By the time I was in high school, I was obese and very addicted to food and sex. I did not date and could not participate in sports and activities. I became increasingly obsessed with sex and lived in a fantasy world while the reality of my adolescence passed me by.

—Jean

I became sexually active way too early and for the wrong reasons. I had an abortion, which I did not want at the time.

—Alice

Repeated acting-out on my part by always being in a sexual relationship with someone. I became pregnant at nineteen and married the baby's father. We are still married.

—Brenda

I never could have any friends over to the house. My self-esteem was so low that I didn't have many friends. I needed braces, weight loss and a lot of other things, but Mother was never able to provide these because she was too busy in her own world. Also, I didn't have a place to call "home" really. We moved all the time with different men she was dating. I didn't feel safe.

—Rose

As a young adult (20+)

I took a lot of chances with my safety. I tried to do whatever anyone ever wanted of me no matter how repulsive it was to me.

—Jackie

Looking for love in all the wrong places in all the wrong ways, broken relationships and now a single mother.

—Amanda

I became very vulnerable to date-rape situations. I was not able to protect myself or voice what I wanted sexually. I was taken advantage of repeatedly and found myself repeatedly enslaved in relationships where the men dominated me sexually. I found it impossible to leave the relationships. Once I even had to move in order to get away from a man who was victimizing me. He was still able to find my new home, and he showed up once again demanding sex. I complied out of fear.

—Jean

I married the first man I saw . . . he was twenty years older than me. I didn't have the courage or self-esteem, or looks for that matter, to find someone my own age. I guess I was looking for a "father figure" because the men my mother provided were far from being a proper image for me. I wasn't strong or able to stand alone. It really didn't matter. We divorced after eight years because I realized that he wasn't the father figure either.

—Rose

I kicked my husband out of the house, almost exactly a year ago, because of his sexual addiction.

—Brenda

Poor marriage choice to a sexual addict because I thought sex was the only true way to express love.

—Sandi

Multiple sexual partners, divorce, remarriage, drinking and drug use, serious impulse control as in money usage, multiple sexual partners between marriages and more drinking between marriages.

—Brian

I learned two months ago that my husband is a sex addict. He kept it hidden for twenty years of marriage. I was so busy being a manager and taking care of our three kids and our life that I didn't even know it. I'm no fool, but he was a master. At forty-one, I'm beginning a journey toward health for the boys and me. My prayer is that he will choose to get healthy, too, but that is the part I can't control.

—Alice

I married a sex addict. I became a severe sex addict myself. I entered counseling, and I attended SAA. My dad's sex addiction brought a lifelong struggle with various sexual issues into my life. Today I am sexually sober, but it took me years to get to the place where I no longer act out compulsively.

—Jean

As you can see, the developmental impact of sexual addiction is quite broad. It can impact you for decades. Of course we are responsible for our choices, and we are now responsible to handle our recovery so we do not continue to pass down a legacy of damage.

Losses, Betrayal and Pain

The other issues that can affect our development are the losses, betrayals and pain we have received along the way. The following remarks from our survey will outline better than I could the experiences of other ACOSAs.

Each one of these ACOSAs has his or her own losses, betrayals and pain. As you read through their tears and anguishes, I hope you can identify known and maybe unknown hurt. Why do you want to do this? Because when you get to the part of healing, you will know what needs to heal.

When you go to the doctor and he asks you what is wrong, you cannot be healed if you say you do not know. Yet if you can tell him where and how it hurts, you can be treated more intelligently. So read on even if it gets difficult. Heal so that you have great things to offer your children and grandchildren.

I have broken the losses and betrayals into two categories: mothers and fathers. Each of us has experienced loss or betrayal differently from different parents. So be brave and continue to keep your heart open to be touched.

Losses from my Father

I lost respect for him and respect for women.

—Bill

My father was distant and not demonstrative toward me with love.

—Brian

The fact that he wasn't there was a loss. He didn't show up again until I was almost thirty. It seems that while my mother was pregnant with me, he was seeing another, and his new woman was pregnant as well. He chose the other woman instead. I never saw him until I was thirty years old. I had no "loss" or "bitterness" against him; in fact, sadly I think of him just like her other husbands . . . just a man who's married to my mother.

—Rose

As a father to me: to know the true meaning of a father/daughter relationship, to never have an opportunity to be a virgin and give away myself, to not be able to see men as God meant me to.

—Amanda

Not available as a father very often, minimal role modeling. I never remember him saying "I love you."

—David

I think we missed out on having a mature relationship until I was in my late twenties.

—Tom

I was not held, cuddled, loved or spoken to kindly. He spent no time with me, nor ever showed any interest in my life. He abused me physically, emotionally, sexually and spiritually. He was not a father. He was a monster.

—Jean

Losses from my Mother

She did not protect or care for me. There was no play or engagement in fun activities. I was only of value to her if I worked. She didn't protect me or my sister from Dad. She was verbally, physically and sexually abusive.

—Jean

As a mother to me I lost protection.

—Amanda

Loving emotionally but not physically. Don't remember any hugs.

—Brian

I lost a mother, but I have a friend . . . I would rather have had a mother all along. She tries not to be a mother, and I resent it.

—Jackie

Betrayal from Dad

He did not support my endeavors or love or cherish me as his daughter. He did not acknowledge me as a human being.

—Jean

The fact that he didn't stay with my mother—he chose to stay with another even when I was first born. Even if he didn't want to be with my mother, he could have and should have recognized me as his daughter and not wait thirty years to do so.

—Rose

Sexual abuse, which continued for many years with different people.

—Trent

Betrayal? He drove me to his friend's house and left me there . . . they abused me. He drove me to a mental hospital when I was fifteen simply because I stood up to his abuse, and he left me there, too! I never went home again.

—Jackie

Betrayal from Mom

I was allowed to do whatever I wanted; I had no boundaries. I think she thought she would lose me, too.

—Brenda

That she seemed to value her sex life more than she valued her duty as a parent. If she were asked this today, she would remember my childhood differently. It's simply something we don't discuss.

—Rose

Her contined denial of the infidelity of my father even though it was well known what he was doing.

—Brock

She didn't protect me from abuse, and she made the choice to abuse me herself.

—Jean

I believe she knew more than she ever let on about his molesting me and my sister.

—Sandi

When Mom met my step-dad, she told of how she believed God brought them together and that since my father was untrue to her, she was free to remarry, and she and my step-dad would set up a Christian home for us. She was untrue to him; the Christian home was in name only.

—John

She betrayed me a lot, but somehow I always ended up forgiving her. She betrayed me when I was nine, and her newest love abused my brother and me. She let me become a foster child rather than sticking up for her children, then she betrayed me at seventeen when she moved away and left me right after I graduated high school. It hurt. In fact, sometimes it still does. We don't talk about it because she gets too upset.

—Jackie

Pain

In this section, we asked ACOSAs to respond to this statement about pain: "The most painful event I have experienced in my parent's sexual addiction was . . ."

Mom's being untrue to my wonderful step-father. God only knows how many other men she had sex with while married to him. I know of one in particular.

—John

Finding letters from my father's lovers and seeing him with a prostitute.

—Mike

My own molestation from my dad, and his lack of approval for me because I wasn't pretty.

—Sandi

It was painful watching my father pursue my friends when I was a teenager. It was painful watching him flirt with various women and engage with my older sister while I was growing up. I was never chosen by him to love, and he let me watch while he sought out others who were more attractive to him than I was. I learned that I would never have what it took to be loved by him.

—Jean

Their divorce and my abandonment from my father.

—Brenda

When my dad told me he had an affair with a woman in a pickup truck in Las Vegas.

—Trent

My father's rejection, first of my mother, then of women in general . . . me included.

—Liz

This chapter may have been difficult for you. It's time for you to do some work yourself. In the spaces below or on a separate piece of paper, write out your losses, betrayals or pain from having a sexually addicted parent.

Losses from my father are _____

_____

_____

_____

_____

_____

_____

_____

_____

_____

_____

_____

_____

_____

_____

_____

_____

_____

_____

_____

_____

_____

_____

Losses from my mother are _____

_____

_____

_____

_____

_____

_____

_____

_____

_____

_____

_____

_____

_____

_____

_____

_____

_____

_____

_____

_____

_____

_____

_____

_____

_____

_____

Betrayals from my father are_____

_____

_____

_____

_____

_____

_____

_____

_____

_____

_____

_____

_____

_____

_____

_____

_____

_____

_____

_____

_____

_____

_____

_____

_____

_____

_____

_____

_____

Betrayals from my mother are_____

_____

_____

_____

_____

_____

_____

_____

_____

_____

_____

_____

_____

_____

_____

_____

_____

_____

_____

_____

_____

_____

_____

_____

Pain I received from having a sexually addicted parent(s) was ___

_____

_____

_____

_____

_____

_____

_____

_____

_____

_____

_____

_____

_____

_____

_____

_____

_____

_____

_____

_____

_____

_____

_____

_____

_____

5

The Impact

The impact of having a parent who is sexually addicted varies from person to person. Your personality, gender, faith, culture, initial beliefs, and exposure to various abuses or neglects are all variables that affect the impact of your parent's sexual addiction on your life.

In this chapter I want you to see how being an ACOSA has impacted others. We will cover several topics, but read each so you are informed about not only how being an ACOSA has impacted you, but also how it may have impacted your siblings.

In our survey we asked ACOSAs to identify ways in which they feel they have been impacted by their parent's sexual addiction. In the following chart you can see the areas in which ACOSAs believe they were impacted due to their parents sexual addiction.

Self-esteem	81%
Spiritually	79%
Emotionally	70%
Socially	71%
Dating	71%
Marriage	69%
Morally	67%
Financially	45%

These are general ideas—and very important ones—but what about specific issues? The following list breaks down the consequences for ACOSAs into several specific areas. I will discuss some of these in more detail in this chapter.

Depression	62%
Eating disorders	38%
Sexual choices	57%
Romantic relationships	64%
Sexual beliefs	64%
Sexual addiction	64%
Sexual anorexia	17%
Marital relationships	69%
Parenting	41%
Financial life	36%

Depression

This is one of the top impacts on adult children of sexual addicts. Depression may impact people differently, but generally the symptoms include:

- Not being able to sleep
- Waking up at night
- Sleeping a lot
- Not enjoying your life
- Feeling worthless
- Decisions are difficult to make
- Weight gain or loss
- Concentration is difficult
- Wishing you were dead

If several of these issues describe you, talk to a doctor or counselor. If you just experienced major grief, some of these symptoms might also be due to your current loss.

Depression for some is chemical or genetic. If you have a family history of depression, it may be a chemical imbalance. If you are experiencing a lot of anger, you can also have symptoms of depression. If you do the exercises in the Healing Path chapter, this should help if the depression is simply a suppression of your rage. Here are a couple of responses regarding depression from ACOSAs.

My depression nearly cost me my life. I spent a total of almost two years in state psychiatric hospitals, and long years afterward recovering my life and getting started again in my education. I am now stable on medication and have largely overcome this problem.

—Rob

I suffer from extreme depression from very early childhood due to my father's abuse and neglect. He made it clear that I was not a chosen woman in his life. He preferred athletic blondes and would flirt with my friends and other young women who fit this type. Since I did not fit the profile, he neglected and rejected me.

—Jean

Eating Disorders

In our survey of ACOSAs, we also asked about eating disorders. An eating disorder can include overeating, binging and purging, or not eating. In our research on wives of sexual addicts, we have found overeating to be a significant symptom of living with a sex addict.

Thirty-eight percent of ACOSAs felt they struggled with eating disorders. Most of these were women.

I began to overeat and hide food from the time I was three years old. I was never held or cuddled by my father, or spoken to by him in a kind way. He was very withdrawn with affection, except he would be overly affectionate with the young women he was drawn to sexually. I used food for comfort and to medicate the pain of his rejection.

—Jean

Sexual Choices

Fifty-seven percent of ACOSAs stated that they believed their parent's sexual addiction impacted their sexual choices, as detailed in the previous chapter.

For most of my youth and early adulthood, I was unable to develop a stable intimate relationship, and all my sexual behavior was solitary and involving behaviors that I had learned in the magazines at home.

—Rob

I ended up choosing relationships with men who were just like my dad. They were very abusive and selfish. I was not able to express my sexual wants, and I did whatever the guy wanted. I felt that sex was the only way to be accepted.

—Jean

Romantic Relationships

The area of romantic relationships was very significant for ACOSAs. Sixty-four percent felt their romantic relationship prior to marriage was impacted by their parent's sexual addiction.

All of my relationships were strictly based on lust and sex for money.

—Bill

Mostly it was about getting someone to really like me. I wanted to prove that I could get the people I wanted. I really wasn't sexually active with many because once I had their interest I moved on.

—Alice

I dated a little, but I never had romance in my life. I was pursued sexually, and there was little interest in me as a person. The men I knew did not treat me with consideration or respect. They did not buy me dinner or small gifts. In fact, they expected favors from me, and they acted as though I should be grateful just to have them around. I was never given flowers or taken on romantic dates. In my marriage, this is still the case.

—Jean

I had three failed attempts to develop an intimate relationship during college years. All three failed due to my lack of knowledge and skill in how to take care of a woman and how to develop appropriate closeness with good boundaries.

—Rob

Mostly very active sexually, and I would find myself bailing out of the relationship when it started getting too serious. I couldn't commit myself to anyone long-term, apart from my first serious sexual girlfriend, who left me about six months later because she has been having affairs with other guys without me realizing.

—David

Way too many of them! Almost always involved sex immediately with guys who were usually very controlling.

—Brenda

Marital Relationships

Relationships appear to be greatly impacted by having a parent who is a sexual addict. What we learned and experienced relationally spills over into our own future relationships. Sixty-nine percent of ACOSAs felt that their parent's sexual addiction impacted their marriage. This is the largest impacted area reported by our group of ACOSAs.

We also asked those in our survey to respond to a statement regarding their marriage. The statement was, "Describe patterns you have duplicated from your parents' marriage." On the following page you can see the responses.

Ignorance and turning a blind eye to inappropriate lust.

—Bill

Married, adultery, divorce, wild postmarital dating scene, married again, troubles . . .

—Jackie

I took care of everything. I nagged about bad behaviors. I thought of myself as a martyr. I chose not to deal head-on with things that shouldn't have been tolerated.

—Alice

Despite the fact that our marriage was founded on Christian principles, and we set out to be different from our parents, we have ended up in much the same place as they did at the end.

—Rob

Blaming each other—trying to look better in front of kids.

—Tonya

Like my father, I try to use sex as a way to feel better, and I've ended up lying to loved ones to cover up my tracks.

—Brock

I find myself mothering my husband by taking care of his basic needs, rather than expecting him to do his own work and care for himself. My husband is immature just as my father is, and he is a sex addict and codependent. I am in recovery, but my husband is not willing to work on his issues. I am a workaholic like both of my parents, and I find myself using money for self-esteem the way my father

*did. I stay up late to avoid sex, just like my mother did. My husband
nags me to come to bed, just like my dad used to nag my mom.*

—Jean

Lying, cheating, raging and abuse.

—Luke

*I married a selfish, controlling man who left me for another
woman.*

—Amanda

*I have continued to view pornography throughout my marriage,
and my wife hates it. I guess I just have this desire that she be more
like my mother and just accept it. However (due to recent develop-
ments), I am glad she has stuck to her convictions and not tolerated
this in my life.*

—Tom

Anger

Anger has impacted each of us differently. For some it was present in childhood or adolescence. For others it showed up in adulthood as anger, rage, addiction or depression. Anger is an issue for
ACOSAs to heal from if necessary so as not to duplicate it in our
marriages or families.

Again we asked the participants in our study to respond to a
statement regarding anger: "Describe how anger has impacted you
due to your parent's sexual addiction." Here are some of their
responses.

*Anger is certainly an interesting thing. Sometimes I think it is a
major problem that needs more control, and other times I don't think
I get angry enough. I let things roll off my back a lot, but I don't want*

to. I want vindication for the pain I have suffered . . . but I don't think I will get it, so I let it go.

—Jackie

I wanted to grab my mother by the neck and ask her, "What the HELL do you think you are doing?"

—John

My anger was turned inside positively. I went to college, earned a degree in a professional field, and now am one of the best in my line of work.

—Rose

I have two-inch-thick armor plating. It used to be one inch thick to protect me from my father's beatings. Now it is two inches thick to contain my rage so that I won't go out and hurt other people. I can have a very cutting tongue. And people who don't know me have backed off very quickly when they have seen anger in my eyes. I was only ever angry once in the boxing ring. I really wanted to hurt the opponent. I hit him twice—the first time raised him about two feet off the canvas, and the second hit him as he was falling. The fight lasted nine seconds, and he was out cold for more than fifteen minutes. They had to administer CPR and hospitalize him.

—David

✳ ✳ ✳

As ACOSAs, we have been wounded. We are innocent in the wake of a crime. We didn't ask to be there as witnesses or internalize messages about ourselves, others, relationships or sexuality.

We have been impacted. We are now responsible to heal. It serves nobody to stay a victim and not grow. I was there, too, so I really do understand the nightmare.

Regardless of your issues, I hope you heal. I so wanted my marriage and parenting to be different from my growing-up experiences. Through the grace of a loving God and loving wife, I say today that the work has been done to minimize any impact of my parent's sexual addiction on my life. You can grow beyond this pain, and I hope you do—you're worth it!

6

Eight Paradigms

Now I want to share eight paradigms I have found that apply to many ACOSAs. These paradigms are not laws of any nature. Rather, they are eight problems I have regularly run into when helping ACOSAs heal from their sexual addiction. I am going to present these paradigms one at a time in an ACOSA group format. These responses are from ACOSAs responding to our survey.

Lead or Follow

I have found that ACOSAs feel comfortable mostly in two areas. First, when they're leading people, be it in business, helping others, social involvement for a cause or at home. Leading is comfortable for the ACOSA. Leading often has to do with control. Listen to our ACOSAs respond to the idea of being totally in control.

This has to be true because if you are not in control, then some-one else is and that is bad.

—Carla

That's the problem. I portray an image as if I have everything under control, and I am a strong person, but in fact, I am less strong on the inside.

—Rose

Although I think I have managed to stay fairly much in control, I feel at risk of losing control much of the time.

—David

I have been a very controlling person, and I have difficulty with perfectionism. However, when it comes to my addictions, I am out of control.

—Jean

In my home now, I am in total control, and I hate not being in con-trol. In fact, my mother has recently separated from my stepfather and is now living with me. She tries to do it all her way here, but I have fits over that sometimes. I don't want it any other way than my way!

—Jackie

The second area an ACOSA feels comfortable in is following others. Fifty-six percent of our respondents stated that they follow others almost unquestionably. Listen in to our ACOSA group as they discuss this issue.

> *I have experienced a tendency to follow authority and to obey leaders even when it seems unjustifiable by their behaviors. I have often picked losing causes to become involved in.*
>
> —Carla

> *I have a pattern of complying with authority out of fear, duty or need. I rarely feel respect for authority, since it's hard for me to trust. However, I follow in order to keep the peace.*
>
> —Jean

Leading and following appear to be the most comfortable places for ACOSAs. The most difficult place for the ACOSA is joining *equally* with others. In our survey, 83 percent stated they have difficulty truly joining others. This inability to join appears to be a major impact of having a parent who is a sexual addict. Listen to their voices echo this idea.

> *I am often a social outcast and feel like I don't fit in. I do not have oneness with my wife because of my selfishness throughout our marriage.*
>
> —Tom

> *I keep a distance from people; I feel like a burden. I have a hard time being vulnerable, or trusting, especially with guys or confident women.*
>
> —Brenda

I had internal depression and anger and never felt alive with others. I only put up a façade.

—Bill

When I have been in classes or at conferences, I have trouble joining in with others. I am more comfortable chatting with the instructors or those in charge than with my peers. I have always felt different and that I am not like other women.

—Jean

I think I am rather reserved with my feelings and level of intimacy to be achieved. I don't know how to truly let go inside of a safe relationship because I have never felt safe.

—Jackie

I have often felt that I was not like everyone else, or that I would be rejected if people found out what I was really like inside. I have often felt that I was so different that others could not accept me unless I were perfect or unless I did exactly what they wanted me to do.

—Rob

Image vs. Closeness

ACOSAs tend to create an image of themselves. Often this is the image they wish was true 100 percent of the time. Unfortunately, ACOSAs are simply human like the rest of us, so the image fills in the gap between the real and the desired image.

This image is real to ACOSAs. They believe it and sell it regularly. Whether the image is success, beauty, confidence, caring, togetherness or other desired traits, they buy it hook, line and sinker. I remember this stage of my own personal healing. It would take my wife hours to convince me that my image was not real. I am not alone. In our survey of ACOSAs, 94 percent needed their image affirmed by others. Here is how our group responded to a question regarding affirmation of their image.

I yearn to hear quite often that I am good at something or that I am loved.

—Carla

I am hungry for praise and affirmation, and I will do ten times the work for someone who compliments me on my performance.

—Rob

I still feel the need for affirmation, maybe even more now than before. I love to hear my addicted husband say that I am all he needs sexually.

—Brenda

I always need approval for my looks and charisma.

—Bill

I need to be affirmed that my body and my looks are still an attraction, and that our relationship is still okay.

—Amanda

Image is easy to maintain. Closeness demands way too much of the ACOSA. Honesty, facing fears, not being in control and being vulnerable to hurt are all necessary to closeness. Image-to-image relationships are much easier to maintain than intimacy. To heal we must be willing to open up that which is not just image.

Trusting Others vs. Trusting Stuff

As you can imagine, trust could be a large issue for ACOSAs. Their environment wasn't consistent; their parents may not have been trustworthy. The information they received about life and relationships was probably faulty as well. In our survey, 94 percent of our respondents stated they had difficulty trusting others. Here is what they had to say:

I believed that all men were lustful animals who always cheat and betray and hurt females.

—Bill

I always expected to be betrayed, whether in friendships or relationships.

—Amanda

I always believe people don't like me and will do all they can to take advantage of me. I am often suspicious of their motives and wonder why I am being singled out for problems.

—John

I am very suspicious of other people.

—Jean

I don't know how to trust, not really. I am trustworthy. I would never hurt a fly, and yet I get hurt all the time. I cannot understand why people are like that. Why would someone hurt someone like me? Why not hurt the bad people?

—Jackie

*[ACOSAs] know they are not trustworthy themselves. And their
parents were untrustworthy. So they do not know where to turn for
real.*

—Luke

Trust no one, and then they can't hurt you.

—Brian

*I have been betrayed so many times and led to feel that I was not
important that I have learned that the only one I can count on is me.*

—Rose

*I have sometimes pulled back from involvement with persons who
may have been good and reliable friends because I felt that I did not
deserve to associate with strong and healthy minded people.*

—Rob

We continued this dialogue about mistrust of others with our participants. Here again, a large percentage (89 percent) stated that
they are suspicious of others and others' intentions. We asked them
to explain their suspicions.

*I always asked my wife why she loved me. I was always suspicious
of her, of anything she did; I read things into her actions that were
not there. I refused to believe this wonderful person could actually
love me.*

—John

*I never believe that someone is truthful with me about their inten-
tions. I always think that someone has an ulterior motive, especially
since my instincts in this are never wrong!*

—Jackie

I have been used for someone else's benefit so long that I question the intent of all.

—Rose

I can never relax in relationships or friendships because I am waiting to be hurt or betrayed or let down when the other person finds out who I really am.

—Rob

I find myself judging others' intentions often.

—Brenda

I question the motives of others. I have trouble with my therapist, because sometimes I don't know why he is willing to keep working with me. I suspect he may have a malicious intent, even though in my mind I know he is a caring person.

—Jean

So if you don't trust people, what do you trust? I have found for most ACOSAs that trusting stuff is much easier than trusting people. Seventy-six percent of ACOSAs in our survey agreed that they find safety in objects. When it came to stuff, this is what our ACOSA group had to say.

Objects cannot hurt you.

—Mike

I am a "pack rat" who collects things and has trouble discarding anything.

—Rob

I wish that was not true but it is. The familiar is calming. It is mine, and I am very protective of my things.

—Carla

I have safety in food. A year ago I was grossly overweight because I would stuff my feelings with food.

—Brenda

I became addicted to food.

—Bill

I keep a stuffed animal in my therapist's office to hold when I feel afraid or troubled. I trust food more than people or God.

—Jean

I think this is very possible. I have a stuffed turtle I bought that I sleep with, especially if I am feeling vulnerable. I like my home with all the little odds and ends arranged exactly as I have them. When people touch my stuff, I get really upset.

—Jackie

When I was a child I always had a rock that I kicked down the driveway to and from school. It was like my best friend, and I got upset when I couldn't find it.

—Amanda

I found comfort in my ability to purchase whatever I wanted. I believed if I could have more things, I would be happy. I'm jobless and cannot pay my debts. My children are supporting me.

—John

After listening to our little group, you can see that trust is an issue for many ACOSAs. You may have to ask yourself about your trust of people versus your trust of stuff as you take your recovery journey.

Knowing Self

To know one's self is a gift. It can take years to push through the image, façade or even what you hope is true about you. Often what we find in the beginning is a wounded self. Over time the self becomes whole, likeable and loveable. This is a real journey for many ACOSAs.

The real self is sometimes elusive to the ACOSA. We asked our ACOSA group to respond to a question about knowing themselves; 86 percent stated that it was difficult knowing their real self. Here is what this group had to say about themselves.

I didn't want to know myself for fear that even I would be displeased.

—Rose

I don't really know what I want or where I'm going in my life.

—Jean

I think I know myself well. It has always seemed obvious where I fell short, but it is difficult to find things about myself that are praiseworthy.

—Brenda

I was lost and seeking approval from strangers.

—Bill

Seven years of therapy, and I still crave to be as secure as my wife is in who she is.

—Brian

For years I have struggled with a sense of identity in who I am, where I am going and what I am doing. I still don't have any clear answers.

—Jackie

Sometimes I don't like who I am and how I behave.

—Brock

I am always trying to be something MORE than what I am. I am always trying to be someone else, someone better, someone smarter. I am never satisfied with simply being ME.

—Jackie

We continued this dialogue with our group of ACOSAs about their real self. We asked them if finding the real person is difficult. Here are their responses.

I hate my real self because if someone really knows me, they won't like me. I truly believe this even though I know it is a LIE!!

—John

I got lost with image, materials and lust.

—Bill

I think the real me is buried under years of destruction, either by others or by myself. I think parts of me are showing, but not the deepest parts. I have so many repressed memories I wouldn't know where to begin to uncover so many years of hurt and pain.

—Jackie

Because we don't even know ourselves, how can we find the real person?

—Luke

For so long I have been someone else that I have wondered if I didn't have many personalities.

—Carla

Living in an atmosphere of secrets and lies, you lose your identity of who you really are, or who you were created to be—a feeling of total loss.

—Amanda

I have been to counselors for more than twenty years, and I still don't feel like I know who I really am—Jekyll or Hyde? Others don't seem to know who I am either.

—David

Emotional and Spiritual Congruence

In the home of sexually addicted parents, many of us have difficulty with emotional and spiritual congruence. We might do better at guessing what we are supposed to feel or believe than actually what we do feel or believe.

As an ACOSA, I want you to listen first to our research participants discuss their difficulty in expressing their feelings. Second, we will hear them discuss their spiritual congruency issues. When it came to identifying feelings, 79 percent stated that they had a difficult time expressing their feelings. Read what these ACOSAs had to say about it.

I would not tell my wife of my feelings because I didn't trust her. I didn't think she'd believe me, plus it was so difficult for me that it was easier to keep quiet.

—John

I can communicate well, but in a truly honest moment, where tensions are high and feelings may get hurt, I will clam up.

—Jackie

I bottle everything up inside of me, and I will not share with anyone unless I know I will receive attention for it, or I know they will not judge me in any way at all.

—Tom

I am aware of my strong feelings, but have a hard time communicating them to others.

—Brenda

I've been taught that my feelings do not matter, so why bother? Also, I fear disapproval of my feelings.

—Rose

I haven't cried for more than twenty years. I have difficulty feeling happiness and joy. My mom died yesterday, and I have hardly felt upset.

—David

I struggle expressing my pain and feelings of anger.

—Jean

Feel as if feelings really don't matter, if you are able to feel at all. Numbness can be the only feeling existing.

—Amanda

As ACOSAs, our feelings are not the only difficult issue. Spirituality is often a journey for ACOSAs. Spirituality eventually has to deal with trust. We already know how difficult that can be. In our survey, 81 percent of ACOSAs stated that it was difficult for them to find true spiritual congruency. So we brought this to our ACOSA group to discuss.

There is not spiritual congruency . . . and much confusion.

—Luke

Trust issues get in the way and the issue of how could God have let this happen, a lot of questioning and distrust even of God.

—Amanda

When you have been disappointed so many times with people you can "see," it is difficult to proceed further in faith with that which you cannot see.

—Rose

I sometimes find it difficult to believe God loves me or that anyone can, for that matter.

—John

Sometimes, I feel that God loves me, but other times, I feel that he doesn't care.

—Jean

I have trouble accepting God's love for me. I feel like I have failed him. I was in my late twenties before I could even accept the reality of God, and then I was very committed for about ten or eleven years. I now feel like I am drifting, still believing and praying, but less committed and lost and without purpose in him.

—David

My parents were hypocrites. Yet they were respected and honored in our church.

—Sandi

I know I am not experiencing all that God had intended for me. I want to. I just don't know how. I want to be able to let go and trust him more. But I think that people only trust God as much as they trust the people they know . . . which isn't very much at all!

—Jackie

I have always been questioning my beliefs and trying to get the Bible to fit my sexual behavior.

—Tom

I have struggled spiritually for years. Now that I am free from my controlling habits, I find it easier to commune with God in a right and intimate way.

—Brenda

Being authentic emotionally and spiritually can happen as you take your journey of recovery. This is work, but the end results are sweet enough to endure the process.

Intimacy Issues

Many ACOSAs have intimacy issues. These show up mostly in a marriage relationship. Ninety-one percent of our respondents stated that they find intimacy with their spouse difficult. We will discuss more of this in a future chapter, but I wanted to give you a sampling of other ACOSAs' experiences with intimacy issues.

I deal with this every day. If I had it my way and my husband would let me get away with it, I would hide in my own little world and blank out everything and everyone. But my husband makes me join life and feel everything. It hurts so bad. It is like a tooth that has an exposed nerve; everything hurts, good and bad.

—Carla

I trusted my children way more than I did either of my wives. Now that my children are adults, I don't trust them anymore.

—John

When we don't love ourselves, and never learned about intimacy from our parents, how can we be intimate with our loved ones?

—Luke

To have true intimacy you must be able to understand some level of what that is. My father was never intimate with my mother; he displayed groping and lust. I don't think he understood it, or was capable of it himself.

—Amanda

I was a stay-at-home mom but realized that I didn't really connect—I was just there.

—Tonya

My spouse and I have no real intimacy. It is all superficial. My children and I are struggling now, too, since they are growing up and discovering life for themselves. I don't like this. I want better than this for them!

—Jackie

Worth More or Less

ACOSAs may also struggle with worth. Their worth as a person or a being is usually in question. The ACOSA tends to have two responses to this worth issue. The first response is overrated worth (43 percent). This is where they believe themselves to be of greater worth than others and tend to compare their strengths to others' weaknesses. The second answer is underrated worth (82 percent). This is when the ACOSA believes he or she is innately worth less than others. Ninety-one percent of ACOSAs stated that they compare themselves to others. Some compare themselves higher than others, and some compare themselves lower than others.

Let's listen in to our ACOSA group as they discuss their overrated worth and how they compare their strength to other people's weaknesses. Sixty-eight percent of ACOSAs stated they were guilty of this type of comparison.

I feel like I am "special" and should be used mightily by God for great ministry. I feel like people should just adore me.

—Tom

I see myself as more than others seem to see in me. I am an artist, but many dealers won't have anything to do with my work. I like the feedback I get from most viewers of my work, but few will buy. Maybe I put too high a price on it because I see more value in it than they do.

—David

To feel better about myself, I would find someone's weakness. Just to say I could do something better gave me worth.

—Brenda

Self-righteousness is an issue for me, and snobbery.

—Sandi

If I am bad at cooking a particular delicacy, I do feel bad, but then I might notice that someone else is hypercritical in their faith, and then I feel better because at least I don't act like that, (even though I am acting exactly hypercritical by thinking this way)!

—Jackie

I look at what I can do and at my good behaviors and compare them to my wife's lack of ability and her bad behaviors (which are extremely mild compared to my bad behaviors).

—Tom

I feel superior if I see that I am stronger in some area than some-one else.

—Jean

As I stated earlier, not all ACOSAs feel hyperworthy. Some ACOSAs feel the opposite—that they are less than others. These ACOSAs (86 percent) tend to compare their weaknesses to other people's strengths.

I find myself as almost never being worth as much as other people. I feel insignificant and unable to function sometimes, and I have a hard time thinking of myself as being as good as anyone else, always less than . . .

—John

I live every day feeling that I don't measure up to others. I always feel that I am in a contest that I am losing.

—Jean

I feel inferior around other men.

—Tom

Always finding someone prettier, sexier, smarter; always wishing to be prettier, sexier, smarter.

—Amanda

I am constantly trying to match the achievements of others.

—Rob

At times I felt like nothing and tried suicide twice.

—Brenda

On the outside, I may overrate my worth . . . on the inside, I often feel worthless—even to God.

—David

We were taught that we were better than everyone else, yet not good enough for Dad.

—Sandi

I am always comparing my failures with successes of others.

—Brock

I always felt less worthy and less capable than others. This drove me to work all the harder to achieve perfection.

—Rob

Regardless of whether you feel overrated or underrated, both need to be addressed in recovery. As humans we have equal worth. Nobody is innately more valuable than another. Feeling equal among people brings so much peace. You are equal in value to all. When you internalize this, you will have made a great step in your recovery.

Give Self Away

The last paradigm I have seen with ACOSAs is their need to give their esteem to others. They will trust others beyond reason and give themselves to an untrustworthy person. In giving themselves away, the zipper is on the outside so that others control their esteem.

In our survey, 83 percent of ACOSAs stated they gave their esteem to others. Eighty percent of ACOSAs stated that they trust people when it doesn't make sense. In addition, 57 percent agree that the zipper of their esteem is on the outside of themselves. Let's listen to our ACOSA group one more time as they make some comments on giving their worth away and trusting the untrustworthy.

I try to treat all people as being better than myself and put myself down in the process.

—John

It's part of who I am. I will bend over backwards to accommodate and uplift someone . . . even one who doesn't deserve it . . . but I never get that in return.

—Jackie

I was ignorant of wrongdoings and turned a blind eye to them.

—Bill

I will "reason" things out in my mind until what someone is saying or doing makes sense.

—Tom

And what about the tendency to allow others to control our self-worth?

I hate being so strongly influenced by others.

—Brock

I don't want to upset anyone.

—Rose

READER/CUSTOMER CARE SURVEY

We care about your opinions! Please take a moment to fill out our online Reader Survey at **http://survey.hcibooks.com**.
As a **"THANK YOU"** you will receive a **VALUABLE INSTANT COUPON** towards future book purchases as well as a **SPECIAL GIFT** available only online! Or, you may mail this card back to us and we will send you a copy of our exciting catalog with your valuable coupon inside.
(PLEASE PRINT IN ALL CAPS)

First Name _____ MI. _____ Last Name _____

Address _____ City _____

State _____ Zip _____ Email: _____

1. Gender
❑ Female ❑ Male

2. Age
❑ 8 or younger
❑ 9-12 ❑ 13-16
❑ 17-20 ❑ 21-30
❑ 31+

3. Did you receive this book as a gift?
❑ Yes ❑ No

4. Annual Household Income
❑ under $25,000
❑ $25,000 - $34,999
❑ $35,000 - $49,999
❑ $50,000 - $74,999
❑ over $75,000

5. What are the ages of the children living in your house
❑ 0 - 14 ❑ 15+

6. Marital Status
❑ Single
❑ Married
❑ Divorced
❑ Widowed

7. How did you find out about the book
(please choose one)
❑ Recommendation
❑ Store Display
❑ Online
❑ Catalog/Mailing
❑ Interview/Review

8. Where do you usually buy books
(please choose one)
❑ Bookstore
❑ Online
❑ Book Club/Mail Order
❑ Price Club (Sam's Club, Costco's, etc.)
❑ Retail Store (Target, Wal-Mart, etc.)

9. What subject do you enjoy reading about the most
(please choose one)
❑ Parenting/Family
❑ Relationships
❑ Recovery/Addictions
❑ Health/Nutrition
❑ Christianity
❑ Spirituality/Inspiration
❑ Business Self-help
❑ Women's Issues
❑ Sports

10. What attracts you most to a book
(please choose one)
❑ Title
❑ Cover Design
❑ Author
❑ Content

TAPE IN MIDDLE; DO NOT STAPLE

BUSINESS REPLY MAIL
FIRST-CLASS MAIL PERMIT NO 45 DEERFIELD BEACH, FL

POSTAGE WILL BE PAID BY ADDRESSEE

Health Communications, Inc.
3201 SW 15th Street
Deerfield Beach FL 33442-9875

FOLD HERE

Comments

I want to be controlled, but then I rebel and fight against it.

—Tom

Self-esteem is usually so low that affirmation becomes my "drug of choice." When another person is pleased with my work, then it only pushes me to do more and more. In contrast, when my work is criticized, it has the opposite effect.

—Rose

I feel nonexistent if no one notices my efforts at work. I get my identity from the way others treat me.

—Jean

One bad mood from anyone close and I am a mess . . . blaming myself or something like that. I don't like bad moods in anyone. But I wish I could have one and let someone try to cheer me up.

—Jackie

I always let how someone else treats me decide how I should feel or act.

—John

We let others control our esteem; we give our esteem to others. If this paradigm fits you, this will be a great place to focus our attention as we go through the recovery process.

❋ ❋ ❋

In this chapter we covered a lot of ground. More likely, all eight paradigms won't apply to you all the time. More likely a handful of these paradigms will need attention and hard work to overcome. I always find that if my clients know the work they have to do, they are more apt to do the work necessary to recover.

Below I have listed the eight paradigms. You can use this as a checklist and progress report. Occasionally come back to this list and see where you have improved. Remember: progress, not perfection.

8 Paradigms for ACOSAs

	Yes	No
1. Lead or Follow	_____	_____
2. Image vs. Closeness	_____	_____
3. Trust Others vs. Trusting Stuff	_____	_____
4. Knowing Self	_____	_____
5. Emotional and Spiritual Congruence	_____	_____
6. Intimacy Issues	_____	_____
7. Worth More or Less	_____	_____
8. Give Self Away	_____	_____

_____

Good Grief

G rief is a natural process that human beings use to naturally move through pain. One painful reality could be the death of a loved one. The pain of that loss is often overwhelming, so the process of grief allows us to take pain in increments or stages.

As ACOSAs, we need a grief process. Not one of us signed up for the painful reality that we "lost" one or both of our parents to sex addiction. Some of you go into a pain reality just thinking about a parent being a sex addict. It is painful. So those who choose recovery go though a process of accepting reality even if it is painful.

Before I help you through the various stages of grief, I want to walk through the three major losses you might have to address as an ACOSA. Remember that to go though the grief process is to be able to accept the facts as they truly are. Many ACOSAs have danced around some pretty significant issues regarding their parents and ourselves.

Loss of a Parent

The loss of a parent to sex addiction is real. You may remember growing up and watching other families and wondering what was wrong with yours. You remember the natural affection a friend of your parents had, but you didn't see that at home. Your addicted parent probably tried to be a good parent at times. There may have been a camping trip or a vacation; he or she may have showed up at major events in your life. But still there was something missing when you looked into your parent's eyes.

Emotional distance or even avoidance is a reminder of your aloneness in this parental relationship, and it is usually coupled with unexplained moodiness due to the sexually addicted parent's guilt and shame over acting out. They were projecting onto you how badly they felt as a parent by guilting, shaming or humiliating you.

For many ACOSAs, there are huge vacuums within your heart and life. The lack of normal development was replaced by the empty philosophy of "if it feels good, do it." And yet for most ACOSAs, there was no talk at all about sexuality. It was as if you were not sexual at all. For some, sexuality became dirty and objectifying.

Many encountered the embarrassment of being a child of divorced parents back when divorce wasn't as common as it is today. Remember trying to explain your stepdad or stepmom to your friends? It took them a while to understand why your real parent didn't live with you.

The addicted parent may have kept pornography to which you were exposed. Some of you were exposed to your addicted parent's lovers, who were introduced as "friends." Many ACOSAs felt really strange inside when meeting them.

The vacuums are endless when one of your parents is a sex addict. It is as if the addiction gets their heart, and you get the crumbs. As you reached adolescence and began questioning the double standards, and the silence or the secrecy, you often paid a price.

Secrets have their own weight. I can't tell you how many children of sex addicts still carry the secrets of the porn, affairs, prostitutes or even sexual abuse from the sexually addicted parent. Inside their heart they know they had a secret so powerful that it could have ended their parents' marriage. How heavy is that for a heart that just wanted to be a kid and play with friends?

Loss of the Other Parent

Not only did we lose the addicted parent, we often lost quite a bit of the other parent as well. The addicted parent, who can't and won't be spiritually and emotionally intimate, often blames and is not intimate with the other parent. So here you have as your primary parent a mom or a dad who is not getting his or her needs met in marriage.

The other parent may have been withdrawn, dysfunctional, overwhelmed, depressed or angry about being recently violated again by the addicted spouse. This is a parent in pain. If you add financial dependency or financial upsets to this mix, especially if it is due to the addiction, this could easily produce a cold, sterile environment.

The demonstrative parent can also look like he or she is the crazy one. The addict shares some more bad news or consequences due to his or her addiction and, whammo, this parent is now throwing a fit.

Non-addicted parents internalize a deep-seated regret of what they have done with their lives and their children. They didn't sign up for a sex-addicted spouse; they signed up for living in a home with a spouse who really loved them and only them. They dreamed of their children experiencing more love than they did as a child, and now their dreams are scared or shattered.

They are still required to function normally—pack lunches, get children to school, do homework and go to work. But no wind is blowing into their sails. Day after day their depletion continues, and they have less to share with you. Many ACOSAs had to hear countless rationales as these parents threw their lives away and wouldn't work, but wouldn't leave either. You may have witnessed codependency and denial to the point it made you angry as an adolescent.

Others reported growing up in a family unaware of the addiction. Then one day the truth came crashing in. Some parents may still appear to be oblivious to what is happening in their marriage. Regardless of how it happened for you, this parent was probably not all he or she could have been had the addiction not been present. The grief over this parent can be harder because of a desire to cling to someone who is somewhat normal so we may be normal one day, too.

Loss of Self

This is by far the most difficult loss to bear. Acceptance of the impact on your life of the pain, manipulation, control, anger, silence, secrets, fears and shame of being raised by a sexually addicted parent and an impacted parent—spiritually, emotionally, sexually, financially, etc.—is extremely difficult. To accept the way things were is to accept not only the pain, but the impact of this pain on your heart as a developing child, adolescent and adult.

A plant doesn't come without needs. Its creator has put in its DNA the desire to thrive. Neither does a child know all that it needs to grow. Most of us know we didn't get many heart needs met growing up. We reacted to these unmet needs and the chaos of our family. We made choices on how to survive this insanity. Some of our choices may have been to hurt others, be addicted, project a more together person than we were. We are clearly responsible for our choices, but not the pain.

We now have to accept that this pain came from our parent's sex addiction. Only then can we grieve the pain of the losses we have experienced. Then we can begin dismantling our defense mechanisms, cleaning up the results of bad choices, and becoming flawed but still loved human beings.

Grief Stages

The stages of grief have been outlined by Elisabeth Kübler-Ross as she worked with those who were dying of cancer. These stages have been applied to many aspects of life such as losing loved ones due to death, divorce or injury and the loss of a primary relationship, such as what ACOSAs experience in their family of origin.

In our survey of ACOSAs, I asked them to identify the various stages of grief they experienced. The results of their grief experiences are in the following chart.

Grief from My Parent(s) Being a Sexual Addict

Shock	55%
Denial	48%
Anger	79%
Bargaining	21%
Sadness	76%
Acceptance	62%

Stage One—Shock

Shock is a feeling you experience when you are initially confronted with a painful reality, such as acknowledging your parent is a sex addict. The first time it was unveiled to you, for a moment, you may have felt a realization of "Oh my God!" That was *shock*. Shock is a feeling that is beyond communication, but you know it when you have experienced it. I have seen many ACOSAs experience this in my office as they discover the truth about their parent's addiction.

During an intake session with my clients, I ask about addictions in their family. They will say something like, "My dad had some porn or affairs or acted out with men or cross-dressed." I'll investigate and put the client back in time thirty years or more, before the Internet, and explain to what lengths they had to go to find a store that sold such things. As we talk, all of the sudden I can see the light come on. "Oh my gosh, he was a sex addict."

It's even more of a shock when we are talking about mothers bringing in boyfriends, or going to bars and leaving children unattended. When the client realizes Mom was a sex addict, it is a real shock.

Shock is a real first stage of grief. Almost everyone will experience this, whether it is Mom filing for divorce, someone was caught in an affair with a prostitute, or a parent is going to treatment. I have had the joy of working with so many ACOSAs who came to me for counseling. Most of the adult children state the shock they felt was real and terrible when they found out that Dad or Mom was a sex addict.

Stage Two—Denial

To deny something means you have a "knowing" on some level that it is true. You can't deny something unless you know there is some validity to it. So denial is a defense mechanism that allows us *not* to see or feel or connect with the truth. For example, if someone died, we might say he or she is not dead. In this case, we would hope that denial would not last for a long time. Unfortunately, in the case of addiction, denials can last for years.

Denial is so great in sexual addiction that it can kill. Sex addicts, who are acting out in populations that are at high risk for AIDS and other communicable diseases, simply say there is nothing wrong with their behavior and they are not going to get sick. This is a defense mechanism that allows them to maintain their addiction.

Many sex addicts have numerous ways of denying their addiction before they reach acceptance of being a sex addict. Some denial statements are: "Everybody does it," "I didn't lose my job," or "I'm not hurting, anybody." Denial is a great way of saying, "I'm not who I know I am." This can be contagious in a family system where everyone agrees that you are a wonderful person and so there is no one to confront your denial.

Family denial of Dad or Mom being a sex addict is sometimes as strong as or even stronger than the addict's own denial. The need for the family to stay together is often greater than the facts. The need for the family to protect Dad or Mom's image can be paramount, and therefore denial comes in handy.

Denial can be essential to surviving your parent's sexual addiction. After all, your parent might be a deacon, pastor, rabbi, schoolteacher or congressperson. You can't or won't believe that someone as good as your parent would do such a thing.

Denial can be amazing. A mistress can call, stop by and even harass a family, and the family just agrees with Dad that she is some pathetic woman needing attention or money. This could happen several times, but the family still believes the addicted parent.

Denial can be a long process that you might go through as the addicted parent marries for the third time. You might have had moments of reflection in which you questioned why things were the way they were, but then dismissed them.

Some of you have had your denial taken away from you like a paper blown by a strong wind when the phone call came about Mom or Dad's affair, Dad getting arrested for exposing himself or soliciting a prostitute, or job losses due to Internet usage at work.

All of these experiences and worse have happened to ACOSAs. Denial can be something we believe so that we don't have to look at our own behavior. This is especially true of the male addict who has an epiphany about his addiction. It doesn't take long at all for him to finally see Dad's addiction as he begins to think over his own life.

The partner (wife or husband) of a sex addict goes through a similar denial-breaking experience. She finds out her husband is a sex addict, and whammo, it hits her like a lightning bolt that her Dad was exactly the same way. *If Dad and my husband are alike, and my husband is a sex addict, then my dad must be a sex addict,* she thinks. The tears roll, and the denial begins to roll away as well.

Most ACOSAs had denial at one level or another; many just didn't have any information. It's only been a little over fifteen years that sex addiction has been around as a paradigm. So most of us didn't have a choice to know in an intelligent manner about our parent's sex addiction.

Denial is a difficult phase of grief. It reminds me of a bumper sticker I once saw: "If you think education is expensive, try ignorance." Those are our options in grieving the losses of growing up in a home of sexually addicted parents. We can educate ourselves, feel the pain, and go through the process—or we can pay the price of denial. In my many years of treating sex addicts, their partners and ACOSAs, I have found denial to be emotionally expensive.

Stage Three—Anger

Anger is a good stage of grief. It means that we are finally interacting with the painful truth. We don't like pain. It is uncomfortable, and we are angry. We are angry that sometimes life has chosen to give us a limitation. We are mad that we can't have the reality of our family like we used to. We are angry that a disease such as sex addiction has cut into our life.

One way I can tell sex addicts are in their grief process is to look them right in the eye and say, "You are a sex addict." Then I ask them how they felt when I called them a sex addict. Many say, "I'm mad."

The same is true of ACOSAs. I say, "You're an adult child of a sex addict." Or "Your mom or dad is a sex addict. How does that make you feel?" Check yourself, how do you feel?

If you are still angry, that is okay; it is a normal stage of grief. After all, you didn't ask for this to be in your family. You didn't ask for the pain, shame or humiliation.

That is the one area of anger you go though in this grief stage.

The other type of anger is over what you did with the pain in your heart. You may have made bad choices regarding relationships, sex, money and much more.

Sometimes the two grief processes run parallel. You can't get angry at Mom and Dad's sex addiction because then you might have to be honest about some of your own shortcomings.

Anger is tricky when you're grieving. If you feel you need help navigating through the stage of grief, you might want to set up a telephone counseling appointment to help you get to the other side. (See chapter 12).

Remember, anger is a good sign when it comes to grief. It means you are starting to process the pain of being an ACOSA. You will go through other stages but accept the stage of anger. If you need help, ask for it; the other side of grief is much less expensive.

Stage Four—Bargaining

Bargaining is a stage of grief that involves an "if/then" logic. For example, "If something hadn't been in my past, then I wouldn't have become overweight," or "If I could stop doing this for thirty days, I wouldn't be an addict." The bargaining can go on and on. It is an attempt to shift the pain and manipulate it to fit into categories but still not experience the full impact of the facts. There is no shame in going through bargaining as long as you know you are bargaining with the pain of your parent's sexual addiction.

Bargaining can be a long process for ACOSAs. You want to believe the best even when the facts are contrary to them. So you start either believing your parent's excuses or you make up some of your own.

"If the police hadn't have set him up . . ."

"If that slutty coworker hadn't seduced him . . ."

"If Dad wasn't so distant, Mom wouldn't have cheated."

"I'm sure that pornography is my brother's."

"I don't know who got on my computer when my parents were here and went to a sex chat room or watched a pay-per-view movie."

"If my parent wasn't such a nice person, people wouldn't hit on him."

"If Mom was putting out, then Dad wouldn't go out for some."

Bargaining is a great way to put off grief for years. After all, you figure out somehow that the addicted parent is less responsible or not responsible at all for his or her behavior.

They feel better; you feel better; there is usually a scapegoat; everyone can be one big happy family—sort of. Bargaining will give you many ideas about how to pass on the fact that your parent isn't a sex addict. After all, if he is sick, what would that make me? I think it makes us ACOSAs, but in the bargaining process it is too early to feel the truth of both the addiction and pain.

Stage Five—Sadness

Sadness is the next stage of normal grief. You have stopped being angry and making rationalizations for your parent's sex addiction. The fact that he or she is sexually addicted is really true. Now you start moving into sadness. This sadness may be over the things lost because of your parent's addiction or over the damages she may have caused. Some ACOSAs think they are perhaps going into depression. It can and may affect you this way. Your eating, sleeping and energy level may be disturbed. If this goes on for a long time, you will need to consult a therapist, but it is normal to go through this stage. You may find some periods of crying unrelated to any significant event. You may feel vulnerable at times. You may isolate yourself from others. Sadness is expected. After all, you have legitimately lost the image of your dad or mom (or both). You may need to rethink and rewrite aspects of your childhood and adolescence. The silence of your parent(s) in large portions of your life is making sense, and it is sad for you.

It is sad to be taunted while growing up with a sexually addicted parent. It is sad to see the impact it has made on the other parent. Sadder still is the impact this secret has had on you, your life, your choices and your relationships. And yet to recover, hope is just one more stage away. Experience the feeling of sadness and understand that it is okay to feel this way because you are close to the end of your grief process. There is no way of getting through the grief process without feeling sadness.

Stage Six—Acceptance

Acceptance is more than an intellectual or philosophical agreement that something is true. Acceptance is an *integration* that something is true. I can cognitively know that someone is dead, but integrating that and behaving as if it were true is a clear indicator that I have truly come to acceptance.

In acceptance, ACOSAs sit up. They can clearly acknowledge two solid facts. First, they can accept that their parent is and was a sex addict. They might be a recovering sex addict, but they are still a sex addict. They don't blame, rationalize, or take an emotional or financial bribe; they just accept the painful fact that "my parent is a sex addict."

The second thing they accept are the choices they made because of the pain of their parent's sex addiction. I had to accept both my parents' obvious sexual addiction. Then I had to accept the choices I made as a result of the pain I was handed. They are not responsible for my choices; they are responsible for the pain.

When I accepted these two painful realities, I was ready to recover from my parents' sexual addiction. I can say without shame or fear that I am an adult child of a sexual addict. I can check how I feel about this, and I am okay inside.

The Eleven Losses

A benefit of going to Twelve Step meetings is hearing others share their strengths, hopes, weaknesses and feelings. I have run partners' groups for wives of sex addicts for years. In hearing them state their losses, I was able to see some losses I didn't see before.

I want to take a minute here and have a mini meeting. I want to share with you some of the things I have experienced as an ACOSA and those I have heard my clients speak over these seventeen years of counseling. We aren't just grieving a lost person; we are grieving the loss of ourselves.

1. The loss of having a real dad or mom.
2. The loss of emotional nurturing.
3. The loss of physical touch.
4. The loss of a parent not impacted by the spouse's addiction.
5. The loss of spontaneous celebration.
6. The loss of innocence.
7. The loss of a soul without secrets.
8. The loss of being heard and valued.
9. The loss of moral training.
10. The loss of healthy sexual training.
11. The loss of esteem.

Reread the chapter on Our Experiences. There, many ACOSAs speak about some of their losses as children, adolescents or adults. These might be helpful for you to see areas of grief you may have to face to heal.

You are worthy to heal from every impact of your parent's sexual addiction. You, like me, have to do some serious work, but I can tell you that it is worth it.

Part of your showing that this is what you are is behavioral. I will behave as if I am a recovering ACOSA and will find the greatest freedom in behaving as who I am, as opposed to trying to create an image or system to cover up what I am. In acceptance, I will accept my parent's sex addiction and other painful events that have happened in my life.

Embracing Grief

Grief is something you will go through in various levels at various times, and so it is important that we look at how we grieve. One way to grieve is resistant. Resistant grief is when we push against the process. We don't want to feel the pain. We aren't praying and asking God to help us grieve or feel the pain. But the more we resist, the longer it is going to take. Grief has no agenda of its own. It doesn't necessarily take one or two years. The approach we take with grief determines how long it takes to go through the process. We can embrace grief and let it take us through the process of healing, or we can resist it and just let it stand by our side until we embrace it.

Embracing grief is coming to a place of knowing that recovery is a process, and that you are going through these stages and embracing them. If you are reading this book, you are probably already out of shock and working toward moving out of denial and possibly further. You are to be congratulated already, and yet there are more stages ahead of you. If you can embrace the process, you can expedite it to a certain degree.

8

The Healing Path

Action is required if we are going to take the pain we have received from others and heal our own wounded souls. It is totally our responsibility to heal our souls. Even if the sexually addicted parent and the other parent went into recovery and became the best example, it would still be our work to do.

Some of the holes inside of us can be huge. Some of these holes come from emotional, moral and spiritual neglect. Many of us have never heard "I love you" or "I'm proud of you" or "You're smart, beautiful or handsome."

Some of the holes are not so passive. The physical, mental and possible sexual abuses experienced are tremendous wounds. Many can still hear the shouting when they close their eyes. They can still see the scenes of Dad hitting Mom, Mom yelling at Dad. These are recordings no child should have as a permanent record on how to treat a spouse or be treated by a spouse.

Some of the holes are sexual. Many ACOSAs have been exposed to inappropriate flirting, pornography or crude statements made about others or themselves. They've been embarrassed and ashamed about what was found in their house.

Most have legitimately experienced trauma, neglect, abuse or all three. These traumas, neglects and abuses are internalized three-dimensionally: They impacted our spirit, soul and body. Our very essence was unpalatable.

Our soul (mind, will, emotions) was there recording the information, responding emotionally, and damaging our very will. Our body was there recording the feelings, storing the fear, hate, anger, hurt and despair. Even if we don't actively remember it all, we were totally present when these events happened to us. In some instances you may remember the room or other factors memorable to the event. If you are feeling something in your body right about now, it's a clue you have some actions to take ahead of you.

Since we are three-dimensional beings, and the trauma, neglect or abuse impacted us three-dimensionally, it only makes sense that the solutions for such traumas would also be three-dimensional.

What I am about to share with you is going to require real work. The results are not found in the process, but the relief afterward is almost instantaneous. Days later, you will feel the permanent work you have completed in discharging your wounds.

I liken it to being shot. When you are shot, the one who shot you is a factor, but the important thing is to get the bullet out so you can heal. Unfortunately, you are now responsible to get the bullet out and go through the process to restore your health.

The pain is present. You are still acting like a person in pain; you utilize anger, addictions, denials or other coping mechanisms. Yet once you pull the bullet out, you can choose to lay your defense mechanisms down. You can heal. Yes, you still have scars, but scars aren't painful.

I had surgery on my right arm many years ago. Right after surgery I was in real pain. I had the kind of pain you scream about. I was wounded, and I was acting like a wounded person. Today, I'm just scarred. When you are scarred, you don't have to flip around and yell at people. People might see the scar, but it doesn't affect you anymore. You can go about your life in a healthy way. Yes, the scar is there, but thank goodness the pain is gone.

There are two stages to the work you will need to do. You will probably have to do these exercises on the wounds from both parents. If you have been sexually abused or raped, you will have to do these exercises on the wounds from each perpetrator. If you are currently in a relationship with a sex addict, you will also have to do these exercises related to this relationship. Each person who caused wounds will get his or her own time in this exercise. Don't lump any of the people together in this process. Do only one exercise per person at a time.

Exercise One: Symbolic Confrontation

In this part of overcoming the traumas, neglects and abuses you experienced, you will symbolically confront the individuals who have wounded you. The symbolic confrontation has four components and all are very important.

A word of caution before you do the symbolic confrontations. If you have heart issues or health issues, consult your physician before doing this exercise.

1. Write an Anger Letter

First, write the name of the person who has wounded you (if you know his or her name) and write this person an anger or rage letter. What I mean is, if you could put this person in a chair, strap him down and gag him, what you would like to say to him for what he did to you in the past? Include the effects it had on your life, your relationships and even your sexuality. Really go off on this person in your letter and don't hold back any thoughts or feelings. Don't worry about your language. This therapeutic letter is never to be seen by the person. Its purpose is for the next part of this exercise.

These wounds have probably affected you throughout your life and kept you from being completely successful. This person deserves the rage you feel about these issues. He or she shot the bullet. Without that bullet, your life and choices probably would be much different today.

2. Warm Up

Get yourself a racquet or bat; most sports stores carry padded bats. Then use a mattress or punching bag to warm up before actually doing the confrontation. Take the bat and hit the mattress or punching bag with small, medium, large and extra-large hits. Do this a time or two to warm up your body.

Then also warm up your voice. Using the same concept while hitting again with small, medium, large and extra-large hits, say the word "no" louder and louder. This may seem awkward at first, but when the rage of your trauma, neglect or abuse comes flowing out of you, you will be glad you warmed up.

3. Read the Letter Out Loud

Now take out the letter you wrote and read it out loud. This is an important part of the exercise. Remember to turn the phones off, and make sure nobody else is home.

As you read the letter, feelings may start welling up inside you; that is normal. The next step will help discharge the trauma.

4. Hit the Object

If you have a mattress or punching bag, go nuts. I mean really hit, yell or kick—whatever you need to do to get the rage, shame and hate out of you and back to the person who wounded you. It's that person's shame you have been carrying all these years, not yours, and it is time to give it back.

This can take anywhere from ten to sixty minutes depending on the trauma and how deeply it's lodged inside of you. You are now taking the bullet from that specific person out of your being three-dimensionally—spirit, soul and body.

The best way I can describe symbolic confrontation is like removing the pus from an infected wound. Once it's removed, the healing can take place. You feel awkward at first, but then more and more comes out. You might feel like you're losing it for a few minutes, but that's okay—lose it! The more you do, the better you will feel afterward.

I have personally done this exercise on people who have wounded me, including males and females, my parents, and others who have attempted to damage my soul. I always feel better afterward. I am able to put a place and time to when I pulled the bullet out, and I begin to heal.

Everyone's experience with this exercise is different. Some feel better immediately, and for others it takes a few days. It's been described to me repeatedly that it feels similar to the feeling you get after you're over a cold or flu, and you realize that you're breathing better again.

For sexual trauma victims, this is a practical thing you can do to clean up the destruction a perpetrator has caused in your life. Go down your list and systematically do this process on one individual at a time. I usually recommend that you give yourself three days in between perpetrators. As you do this process with each perpetrator in your life, follow the same four steps to a symbolic confrontation.

Exercise Two: Symbolic Releasing

Now that you have completed step one with the symbolic confrontation, this second exercise is going to be more about releasing yourself from the people who have wounded you.

In this exercise, you will need two chairs and, again, some privacy. Turn off the phone, and make sure everyone is out of the house or asleep before starting. In this exercise, you will take the two chairs and have them face each other. There are three phases to this exercise. I will walk you through each.

Phase One

In this part of the exercise, you will sit in one of the chairs. We will call this Chair A.

In chair A you will role-play as the person who hurt you. If the person who hurt you was named Fred, use his name. If he or she was a stranger, you can give him or her a name or simply use "I am the one who abused you." Let's stick to Fred for our example. In chair A you role-play as Fred. As Fred, you can apologize and ask for forgiveness. Be specific during the owning of the abuse or neglect. Don't just have Fred say "I'm sorry." If Fred was an adult and hurt you, be specific. As Fred, say, "I am the one who hurt you by . . . I hope you can heal, and I ask you to forgive me."

So in chair A you will role-play as the person who hurt you and state what he or she should say to you for what was done and what it cost you. You are talking to yourself symbolically in chair B.

Phase Two

After the person who has hurt you has appropriately apologized, then physically get up and move to chair B. In Chair B, you will now role-play as yourself. You have just heard the person who hurt you (Fred) apologize and ask forgiveness for his acts toward you and the effects they had on you.

In chair B you can respond any way you wish. You may not be ready to release him or forgive him. Whatever your thoughts or feelings are, verbalize them to the person who hurt you. The purpose of this exercise is honesty. Releasing this person is a gift you need to eventually give yourself. His life moved on whether you forgave or released him or not. But releasing him or forgiving him doesn't mean that you approve of what he did to you. You are simply releasing that behavior from having any influence in your life.

If you are unable to forgive or release the person at this time, try again in a month or so for your own sake. If, however, you are able to forgive or release him, go now to phase three.

Phase Three

In this phase you will now physically move back to chair A. You are going to resume the role of the person who hurt you (Fred). As this person you respond to the forgiveness or releasing (if it took place) that has been extended to you. After the person who hurt you responds to being forgiven or released, you are finished with the symbolic releasing.

This is a powerful exercise for most ACOSAs. As you do this exercise, you can say good-bye to this chapter of your life. Most ACOSAs from this point can integrate the trauma event as part of their history without all the ongoing effects, much like having a scar from an accident but no longer having the pain.

✳ ✳ ✳

I hope all of you reading this who need to heal from your trauma, neglect and abuse do the exercises that were outlined. These exercises have changed thousands of men's and women's lives over the years. You can apply them to other traumas as well.

As ACOSAs we can break the cycle of pain and hurting other people. We can do the exercises mentioned, dislodge the bullets of trauma, neglect or abuse, and begin to heal.

Once we are in a healing place, we won't act like the rest of our hurting gene pool. We now value others and ourselves. We make better relational, financial, spiritual, emotional and sexual choices. We don't have to be one of the walking wounded.

I prefer to be the walking scarred. Yes, all this abuse, neglect and trauma has happened. Yes, I took responsibility to heal from these wounds, and yes, I am free now to give and receive love; it is what I was truly born to do.

Please go for it! It is work, but you will never regret the effort you put into your healing. The impact it has on you, your families and the families that follow is so worth facing the pain of your life today.

9

Sexual Wholeness

One of the largest impacts of having a parent who is a sexual addict is on our own sexuality. Both sons and daughters of male and female sex addicts get some pretty bad messages about sex.

Most of the misinformation that ACOSAs receive is that sex is one-dimensional. Sex addicts are often connected to an object reality of sex, not a relational reality of sex. Their neuropathways have been connected to fantasy and objectification of people and not to the souls of people.

So with bad information from parents and a "learning as you go" philosophy, there might be some gaps to keep you from having sexual wholeness. I want to cover a few principles to walk you toward sexual wholeness.

Heal the Past

All of us have a sexual history. Even if you haven't had sex, you have a sexual history. As we discussed in the Our Experiences chapter, many of us have sexual issues. For some, it is not being able to initiate sex; others have difficulty enjoying sex or orgasms.

Some ACOSAs have difficulty being emotionally or spiritually connected during sex. Some have used fantasy during sex. Some have active sexual addiction or sexual anorexia issues. Some ACOSAs have sexual abuse issues to overcome.

The first step toward sexual wholeness is to clean up your own issues. You might be tempted to clean up your spouse's issues. But if you clean up your own stuff, it can make it more obvious to your spouse what his or her issues might be because you are being much healthier sexually.

First, get informed. If you read the Our Experiences chapter and still need more information on sexual addiction or sexual anorexia, please get the information you need. If you are a sexual abuse survivor, I recommend that you do the cleaning house exercises mentioned in the Healing Path chapter. After you complete the anger work on each sexual perpetrator, move to the forgiveness exercise.

Second, if you need to get into a support group for sexual addiction, sexual anorexia, partners of a sex addict or a sexual abuse recovery group, please do so. If you can't find one, consider a teleconference group run by a therapist. You might need support to become sexually healthy. Please give this gift to yourself.

Third, many ACOSAs have a great deal of shame about their sexuality. Some shame is related to what was done to you. Other sexual shame is related to sexual behaviors that you participated in or watched or fantasized repeatedly about. You might consider some counseling on these issues. I will go over the guidelines for finding a counselor in the Professional Helpers chapter.

You are going to be sexual until death. You can be sexually healthy or sexually dysfunctional, and that is the choice you get to make. It is similar to money. You will have financial issues until death. You can choose to be financially responsible or financially irresponsible, but you are still financially oriented. I hope you choose the path to sexual wholeness. It is a lot of work, but the results are absolutely mind-blowing.

Fourth, you are going to need to be honest. You can't be sexually whole and keep big secrets. If you cheated on your spouse, talk to a therapist before you choose to disclose. I'm not talking about just being honest about possible infidelity. I'm talking about being honest about being sexually selfish, not giving of yourself, not initiating, or being demanding, critical or involving your partner in pornography or acts that were uncomfortable for him or her. You will need to find a place to make your sexual amends.

Remember, if you are married, you are going to have sex thousands of times with your spouse. Heal the past so your future sexuality together can be whole, free and connecting to the point of satiation for both of you.

3-D Sex

I think "3-D," standing for three-dimensional sex, is probably the best paradigm for sexuality there is. Sex is one of the few things we do that engages all of who we are—our bodies (boy, do they look different during sex), our souls (mind, will and emotional process are definitely on overload) and our spirit (that inner part of us that can serve and experience beyond words and touch).

I want to walk through three-dimensional sex and give some practical tips on how to be sexually successful in a three-dimensional way for the rest of your life. If you're going to have sex, you might as well go all the way, right?

I often tell my clients, you can have squirt-gun sex (one-dimensional) or you can have atomic-bomb sex (three-dimensional), the kind that blows out your body, soul and spirit. Another way of saying this is you can have bronze-, silver- or gold-medal sex. I say go for the gold!

Now most ACOSAs are not informed about gold-medal sex. As an ACOSA, most of the sexuality you learned at home doesn't include three-dimensional sex.

So we travel this new frontier. For some it will be a visited place a few times in your life; for others (and I hope for everyone reading this book) it becomes a familiar place. I figure you only live once, and you might as well have the best of everything you can, including sex.

Body Sex

Body sex is important. Without the equipment for the process, it would not be possible. When we have sex, our body is one of the three major contact points of our sexuality. When sexual, our bodies go through incredible changes just so we can have the absolute maximum pleasure. When we were engineered, a lot of time was taken to make sure our bodies would have as much fun during sex as humanly possible.

During a sexual release, we receive the highest level of endorphins and enkephlines in the excitement centers of our brains. This gives sex the biological kick that keeps us coming back for more.

The body is one dimension of the three dimensions for sex. Unfortunately for some, this is the only dimension of sex they experience. I cannot even count how many women in my office have told me that this is all their husband or significant other thinks sex is.

I'm not talking about the couple that has a quickie, the scratching-the-itch type of sex. Most couples experience that, and as long as that's not the majority of sex, it is fine.

But some ACOSAs can go no richer in their sexual experience

than body sex. For some, their souls and spirits are so stuffed down inside that they can't even access them during sex. Some ACOSAs who can't go deeper are stuck in a disconnected fantasy state, or they disconnect during sex because of other reasons, such as sexual abuse.

Whatever the reason, when a person experiences only body sex, his or spouse feels empty, and over a period of time sex becomes less satisfying. Somehow women (mostly women) intuitively understand 3-D sex and yearn for their souls and spirits to be touched, too. When this doesn't happen and their husband can go no deeper, they have less and less desire for just body sex.

Soul Sex

Every person has a soul. Each person's soul is totally unique to him or her. All souls have three areas or realms: the mind, the will and the emotions. In 3-D sexuality, all three realms are involved. The mind definitely is involved in receiving and giving stimulation and recording all visual stimulation. The will to serve and be kind is also online during sex. Emotions are especially involved.

Emotions are the last aspect of our soul. Now here is an area where our culture, religion, education and even families have left most of us underdeveloped. I was not trained in my emotional realm during high school, college, graduate school or even in my doctorate program, and I specialized in psychology! I remember specifically thinking about this when I was working on my master's in marriage and family counseling. Although they were talking about feelings and their importance, not one class or professor was teaching me how to have or communicate my feelings.

I knew I was underdeveloped in the emotional areas. In my family, we were allowed three feelings: angry, really angry or what I term "other." Other meant "leave me alone. I'm going for a walk, a drink or something else because I don't have a clue what I am feeling." I was truly emotionally constipated in my teens and early twenties. It's like I had hundreds of feelings but only three doors from which they could emerge. So if I felt hurt or rejected, I chose anger or "other" so I could blow up or leave. If I felt unimportant or unsuccessful, I could choose really angry or angry. You get the point; it wasn't fun being around me because I was emotionally underdeveloped.

To have complete soul sex or two-dimensional sex, body and soul, your soul needs to be fully developed in all three areas: mind, will and emotions. In the next chapters I will give you practical tools to "open the doors" and do this on a daily basis with your spouse.

Soul sex is when you can skillfully bring thoughts, feelings and your willingness to express your love, commitment and the cherishment of your spouse to your sexual experience. When your spouse feels the powerfulness of your full soul, and you're also fully present in your body during sex, you both feel much more connected, closer and, I might add, satiated.

Like I said, it takes some time to develop the emotional side of your soul, but that's not asking much to be more sexually whole for yourself and your spouse. The great thing about gaining new skills is that once you have them, you can have them for life.

Spirit Sex

The spirit is the deepest part of a person. The spirit in us is much deeper than thoughts or processing information. It's intuitive. It sees beyond what we experience physically, verbally or even logically. It's that part that kicks in to tell you somebody is lying to you or if you can trust someone. It's that part that connects to the bigger scheme of things. It's the part that awes when viewing the ocean or mountains, or the first time you hold your child. It's the core of who we are. It is our connecting point for both our earthly relationships and for the spiritual relationship we choose to have or experience.

I don't mean religion here; I mean spirituality. This is the deepest part of you that can reach out to the person you love in times of great joy and great pain. It's that part of you that can reach out to the God of your understanding. It is your essence. It's the part of you that operates and is experienced beyond words.

Your spirit can truly connect with your spouse. You feel a one-ness not just of body and soul, but of spirit. It truly feels as though the two of you have become one, essence to essence connecting. When you connect your spirits you are going to experience sex as almost a life-changing experience.

Three-dimensional sex is the absolute sweetest and most satisfying sex I have ever experienced. It touches me so deeply that I am completely satisfied and sexually content. This is sexual wholeness at its true height. It's not just an orgasm; it's an internal three-dimensional body, soul and spirit explosion. That's real sex! That's the experience you can have regularly with your spouse if you'll take the time to develop spiritually and emotionally. I will cover the practical side of this in the next chapter. In just weeks you can bring this type of connection into the bedroom on a regular basis.

Living in Colorado has taught me something very important. If you're willing to climb the mountains, you get to experience the incredibleness of the mountaintop view. If you're not willing to climb, all you get are the pictures and stories of others. I don't want pictures and stories; I want the real thing, and I hope you do, too.

Tips for Better 3-D Sex

Before I close this chapter, I want to leave you with three tips that will help you to begin to experience sex in a 2-D and 3-D manner. You can start these tips today, and as you use the skills from the next chapter your sexuality will become incredibly whole.

These tips are for when you're actually making love to your spouse. They may feel different or awkward at first, as all new skills do, but stick with them a month and you will never go back.

Tip One: Eyes Open

It is said that the eyes are the windows of the soul. I couldn't agree more, especially during sex. Your spouse needs to see your eyes, and you need to see his/hers during sex. When you're making love, don't close your eyes and disconnect. It looks funny, but keep those eyes wide open, and ask your spouse to do the same, especially at orgasm. Your explosion will be experienced by both of you. Your connection to his/her soul and spirit will be so natural. And what you look at when you release is what you attach to. I can honestly tell you I have been doing this over sixteen years, and my wife's eyes totally turn me on; her soul gets me sexually turned on and she knows it.

Tip Two: Lights On

When making love, keep a light on. It can be candles, a small lamp or even light from an adjacent room. You need light so you can see your spouse. Remember, it's what or who you are looking at when you release that you bond to.

Tip Three: Nurturing Conversations

When making love, the words you say go deeper into your spouse than at any other time that you communicate. What you say to each other will be deeply recorded in your soul for days or weeks.

If you are giving affirming words during sex, these words go deep into the heart of your spouse and will be kicking around in his or her heart and mind during the day when you are not around. I think you get the point. What is said during sex is said to the heart.

Utilize this time. Do not offer dirty talk or use criticism, or it will backfire. Invest words of praise into their being at this time, and you will connect at the deepest levels and satisfy each other intensely.

Imagine hearing words during sex that affirm your sexuality while making love to your spouse. If you show nurturing during sex more often, it comes back to you.

10

Intimacy Ever After

For ACOSAs, intimacy is rarely a strong suit. Intimacy issues are very common among people from addictive families in general. It makes sense that a sexually addicted parent will not be able to role model a connection with people. The addict connects to stuff, not people, until he or she enters recovery.

Throughout this chapter I will be discussing intimacy in marriage. If you are married, or on your way to being married or married again, make sure you have these skills. They will help you connect spiritually and emotionally, which will also help you in becoming sexually whole.

Throughout my years of counseling couples, I have found that many marriages have no structure that encourages intimacy. We grow up believing that we get married and live happily ever after. Yet we are often not equipped for intimacy and can be disappointed when our husband or wife doesn't possess the secret code to intimacy either.

The early part of marriage can often be fun as you begin to learn about your spouse, go to work or school, get your first apartment, pick out furniture, go to church, and are physically intimate without guilt. The new complexities of life, along with the multitude of new decisions, can keep couples talking and sharing regularly.

Slowly and subtly—no one really knows when or where it happened—something changes within the relationship. You don't seem to talk as much. Decisions are not met with the same glee as when you were first married, but instead they are delegated, and then discussed. Purchases become fewer; sex and life begin to take on a certain level of routine. You don't feel as close and seem to be just living together. What happened? How did the passion for each other leave?

Many couples lose their priorities. Passion is a result of priorities. Americans think passion is either a part of them or it isn't. But passion is a dividend of consistent investments placed into a relationship.

Let's go back a minute to when you were dating and starting to think that being married would be a good idea. Remember the passion in life that you had for your future spouse? Of course, you remember the passion, but what you may have forgotten is the foundation of that passion, the *priority* of the relationship.

Do you remember how you "made" time to be together? You planned your days and weeks around each other's work schedule, including days off. Those of you who were like me and moved away from a future spouse to go to school have the phone bills to prove it. Those phone bills took a good portion of the little income I made just to tell her about my day.

Do you remember the gratitude you had for the smallest things your future spouse did for you? This was especially true if my future spouse cooked for me. I was so grateful! You offered a constant stream of praise for your future spouse. Do you remember when you thought your future mate was so smart and attractive and had so much potential? You believed in him or her and offered regular encouragement.

Passion is a result of priorities. So many people try to get the passion back instead of getting their priorities back. Once you get the priorities back, the passion naturally follows and grows. Most couples ask, "What priorities?" I will discuss these priorities shortly, but before I do, I want to share an analogy I often share within counseling sessions to ACOSA couples. Many couples who come in for help in their marriage have sprains or fractures in their relationship. I liken the repair of this marital relationship to a fracture or broken bone. When you break a bone, you can still function but you look and act funny. Then you go to the doctor or emergency room.

The first thing they do is x-ray the bone in question. They look at the structure. Regardless of how it happened, the x-ray shows a damaged structure (your bone). The doctor and nurse apply a structural treatment to your structural problem, most likely a cast.

The cast is a structural treatment. The cast itself is just plastic or plaster; in and of itself it has no healing properties. But when it is applied to a broken bone to hold the bone in place, surprise! Healing can and does happen.

That is what placing the priorities back into a marriage can do. No matter how sprained or broken, healing can and does take place. I have seen literal miracles in restored marriages when priorities were put back into the relationship. One of the structures I apply is what I call the "three dailies."

The Three Dailies

I want to add a personal note of testimony. I would never ask you to do something that Lisa and I have not done or are not doing

presently in our relationship. Two of the three dailies Lisa and I
have done every day (with only a few exceptions) for well over
seventeen years. When I developed the third exercise, we also
actively applied this to our marriage.

Lisa and I maintain our relational priorities by practicing these
three exercises. They are part of our bedtime routine. Neither of us
expects to go to sleep without our relational ritual of the three
dailies.

I can tell you this is a major highlight of my day. I get to hear
about my wife's day and hear her heart, and she gets to hear about
my day and heart as well. This relational structure has richly developed our skill for intimacy to such a level that it can weather the
day-to-day challenges of children, writing and media demands,
along with all of the other commitments life demands of us. When
incorporating the three dailies in your marriage, priorities are
restored and consequently passion is restored. There is not one person who knows me on any level who is not aware of my passion for
Lisa. I love her, and really like her as well. This passion is the fruit
of discipline that is born out of a heart of love.

I am a recovering child of a sex addict, abuse survivor and a
recovering addict. I have every excuse not to have intimacy. But I
believe in intimacy ever after. I chose a path of developing skills my
sexually addicted parents didn't have to give me. I take responsibility to be intimate.

You can have intimacy ever after if you are willing to work for it.
Intimacy is an applied set of skills, not something mystical. When
you apply the skills, you will get the same happy results I have
received for these many years of marriage.

Daily One: Prayer

Prayer is an absolute necessity in your marriage. I am constantly
amazed when recovering couples tell me that the last time they
really prayed together (not including praying over food or a good-
night prayer with children) was years ago. Usually their rationale

goes something like this, "We both pray, just not together." That's fine, but I really don't see how that can in any way be optimal.

Prayer is standard in recovery. One alcoholic was talking to his sponsor about this prayer thing. He said to the sponsor, "I don't believe in God." The sponsor replied, "I didn't ask you to believe in God; I asked you to pray." Recovery is so much of doing the right behavior first and the rest follows.

I'll never forget a sex-addict client I had in Texas. He was agnostic, but agreed to pray. Weeks later he came in with story after story of how his prayers were answered. He said, "I don't know about this God thing, but this prayer thing really works."

Prayer is one of the priorities that must be set in place by a couple desiring more intimacy. Remember intimacy is three-dimensional—spirit, soul and body. As we grow spiritually together, our intimacy in the other two areas will grow as well.

Prayer is just talking out loud to God with your spouse, similar to talking with a friend. Prayer doesn't have to be hours-long or in any particular position. The principle of connecting with God together is essential.

I know better than most that each spouse and couple has many variables. Some of these differences include sleep preferences, work schedules, children's school and extra curricular activities.

Look at your schedules. When can you pray together: in the morning, at lunch or in the evening? Take the time to discuss this with your spouse and see if you can agree on a time or two to pray together.

Now remember, this is a daily exercise. Those who travel a lot often ask me what they should do about praying when they are out of town. In this day of modern technology, it really has become a nonissue for the creative person. You can use your calling card or mobile phone and pray with your spouse on the phone. This really demonstrates a commitment to maintain your spiritual intimacy. Even if you're in Hong Kong, you can send an e-mail with a prayer to your spouse. Remember that the *structure* first brings healing, then passion, then belief. As you walk together spiritually, your intimacy will flourish.

I love walking in the garden of my life with Lisa and bringing her into the presence of our loving God. I really believe this has been instrumental in developing the strength and intimacy of our marriage.

Daily Two: Feelings

Emotional intimacy is a second very important aspect that couples need to develop and maintain throughout their relationship. Often early in the dating relationship and in our early marriage, we readily share our feelings about life situations, people and our dreams. Many don't know what happened to their feelings when they got married, but for many couples they appear to go into hiding. Life gets more complicated, and your conversations seem to get more managerial, such as who does this or how is that going to get done.

Marriages can be managed and function well and yet still not have the connectedness you once had. Eventually in your marriage you can begin to feel alone, unsupported and not understood, wondering why you are even going through the motions. These feelings are common among couples who don't have an emotional structure in place.

Emotions are an important part of who you and your spouse are. Emotions are very much a part of your spouse's personality and influence how he or she processes life events all day long. Remember that many couples don't see each other for eight to ten hours of the day. Your spouse has been in the big bad world. People or situations all day long have positively or negatively affected his or her heart.

We seem to be intuitive about talking to children when we ask them about their day. We don't just want the facts, but want to know what their heart has been through that day.

When I talk with couples about expressing feelings, it is often apparent that they have limited skills or points of reference. I can totally empathize. Even though I had hundreds of feelings, I only had three major doors of communication. This gets really fun if you marry someone with the same three doors. If you felt unimportant, you may express it by feeling mad, really mad or other. If you choose to be angry but your wife feels frustrated because of her day, she may choose to pick "other." In this scenario, "mad" is talking to "other" instead of "unimportant" talking to "frustrated." I'm sure you all have been there, where the feelings that were being expressed didn't line up with the real feelings the person was having.

We all come with many feelings as standard operating equipment from our maker. The problem isn't that we don't have feelings. The problem is the limitations that we have in the skills to express them. I know I was emotionally illiterate when I was first married. I had lots of feelings, but no skills to identify or communicate them to my beautiful bride, Lisa.

Even while getting my master's degree in marriage and family counseling, I still wasn't receiving skill development in the areas of identifying feelings or communicating them, and so I took it upon myself to learn this skill. What I realized is that most of life is about learning skills.

Let me give you an example. As a youth, I learned nothing about fixing cars. So even as an adult, lifting the hood of a car was shaming for me. No matter how many degrees I have, I still had no mechanical training or skills. If I were to take a course in basic mechanics and learn these skills, I could become skilled at fixing a car.

That's what identifying and communicating feelings is—a *skill*. Skills can be learned by anyone. I can testify to that personally as well as anyone. I have witnessed many couples who have grown in the skills of identifying and communicating their feelings.

I have seen husbands and wives move from emotional illiteracy to emotionally communicative competence. I have countless memories of couples taking their first stab at practicing the feelings exercise that we will be discussing momentarily. They slowly do their first one or two feelings, and as they practice this daily these couples begin readily talking about their feelings to each other and me. Their ability to do this is critical for intimacy.

If you can't share the feelings in your heart because of a lack of training and practice, how can you expect a heart-to-heart intimacy to occur? If you have been able to skillfully tell your spouse what you feel and what is in your heart, then your spouse must likewise be able to clearly communicate his or her heart to you.

This lack of skill is one of the largest hindrances for a couple to start or maintain intimacy. That is why the feelings exercise is critical over the next few months. I do want to warn you that this is an exercise, and therefore it does require some effort to get a degree of mastery.

Many adults have had to learn the computer. I liken the feelings exercise to learning a new computer program. At first, it feels unfamiliar and awkward. Over time the learning curve feels a little less formidable. Then, before you know it, you have figured it out, and you begin to feel a little more confident. Finally, you ask yourself, *How did I ever live without this?*

Life is funny that way; some of the best things in life take effort to achieve. If you plant corn, you get corn later in the harvest season. Likewise, as you sow emotional intimacy, in time you will reap emotional intimacy.

Wouldn't it be a great day indeed if you, deep down in your heart of hearts, knew that you were completely heard by your spouse and that you were accepted? This kind of warm fuzzy only comes after time and practice.

The following exercise is designed to increase your ability to share your feelings with others. This is a skill every ACOSA can benefit from.

THE FEELINGS EXERCISE

The feelings exercise is relatively simple. Pick a feeling from the list in appendix B of this book. Place the feeling word within the following two sentences.

1. I feel _____ (feeling word)
   when _____.

2. I first remember feeling _____ (same feeling word) when _____.

Example 1:

1. I feel **adventurous** when **I take my wife and two children hiking up the mountains in Colorado Springs.**
2. I first remember feeling **adventurous** when **I was about thirteen years old, and my mom bought me a ten-speed bike that I rode all over town.**

Example 2:

1. I feel **calm** when **I can be alone in nature and sit really still for a short while.**
2. I first remember feeling **calm** when **I was first taken out of foster homes, and my mom gave me a stuffed animal that I could sleep with.**

I think you can get the idea. In the first sentence you pick whatever feeling you want and give a present tense example of the feeling. In the second sentence you use the same feeling word but choose an early experience, usually from childhood or adolescence.

It is the earlier feeling that can be difficult. Do not cop out and give an example from a year or so ago. Really think hard and do the exercise correctly. Some men and women who have had difficulty remembering a feeling from the past have found it easier if they start with a past memory during childhood and attach a present feeling to that experience. For example, those having difficulty might go to a childhood experience where their mother or father forgot to pick them up from school one day. One of the feelings they might feel was alone because everyone else left on a bus or was already picked up. Then come up with an example of feeling alone in the present, such as "I feel alone when I am on hold on the phone for a long period of time."

I also want to warn you against two things with this exercise and then talk about boundaries for your feelings exercise. The first thing you don't want to do with this exercise is to use the same feelings word over and over again. This really serves no purpose and will not give you or your spouse the desired effect for developing intimacy. The second thing you don't do in this feelings exercise is to use one childhood example for twenty different feeling words. Consider the above example of the person being left at the school. Don't give this same example day after day with different feeling words such as abandoned, helpless and confused. Although these feelings may be legitimate for one example, it would not serve you or your spouse well to just keep pumping one experience over and over again when your life is full of experiences. As I have said before, it may be slow going at first, but even childhood experiences become easier to remember when you practice the feelings exercise.

I have developed some guidelines to be used while completing this exercise. The following guidelines will limit or remove some obstacles that couples have experienced within this exercise. Please follow these, and it will make your experiences much more positive.

Feelings Exercise Guidelines

Guideline One: No Examples About Each Other. You can talk about feelings that include one another at any other time of day, but *not during the feelings exercise.* It is very important not to violate this guideline.

The feelings exercise is designed to be a safe place for both the husband and wife to open their hearts to one another. If you start using the exercise to say "I feel frustrated when you don't pick up your socks," the exercise will become unsafe and will dissolve. You can feel frustrated about traffic, your children, the dog or anyone other than your spouse during this exercise.

This guideline also applies to positive feelings about your spouse. Suppose you use the word "cuddly." Again, you can feel cuddly with the children or the dog, but don't use your spouse in the example during the feelings exercise.

This guideline is very important in order to keep the exercise alive and provide you both with a way to learn and maintain emotional intimacy. If your spouse inadvertently starts giving an example that involves you, kindly remind him or her that it doesn't count and to give you another example. If your spouse continues to violate this principle, I would question the intent. My experience is that those who sabotage this exercise don't want intimacy. They might say they want intimacy, similar to the fact that they would like to be a millionaire, but if they don't work for it they truly don't desire it.

"How should we choose our feeling word?" is a frequent question I hear from couples working on their feelings exercise. I warn couples about just going down the "A" list because it can be very difficult to start with words such as "abandoned," "aching" and so on. The truth is that it really doesn't matter how you or your spouse pick your individual feeling words.

Some couples just close their eyes and pick one from the list. Some pick one feeling word that starts with "A," and the next day they pick a feeling word that begins with "B" and so on. Others just pick a number, such as nine, and do every ninth feeling word. Some just choose a feeling from that particular day. Again, the method each person chooses in order to pick his or her feeling word is not relevant to developing and maintaining intimacy.

Another commonly asked question from couples is, "How many feeling words should we do a day?" I recommend two feeling words a day per person. So the wife does a feeling, then the husband does his. Then the wife does her second feeling, and the husband does his second feeling. Then you're finished with the feelings exercise. Remember to follow the guidelines to ensure you get the optimal benefit from the exercise.

Guideline Two: Maintain Eye Contact. The second guideline to completing your feelings exercise is to look each other in the eyes while sharing your feelings. Looking each other in the eye is important as intimacy is beginning to take place. There is so much truth in the old saying that "eyes are the windows of the soul." When we look into another person's eyes, we can see them.

So many ACOSA couples grow apart and have a difficult time

even remembering the last time they looked each other in the eye for more than a few seconds. I have seen both husbands and wives have difficulty looking each other in the eyes while doing the feelings exercise. They have become so used to talking at each other instead of to each other. They look at the floor, the ceiling or past their spouse. Jokingly, I say, "That was great to share that feeling with your shoe. Now let's try it again and share it with your spouse." We all laugh, but the spouse has to do this feeling over and over again.

In my office, when a couple does the feelings exercise, I watch so that I can observe their eye contact and see if they are maintaining it throughout the exercise. After a few attempts, most couples can maintain eye contact as they share their feelings. Once again, this is an important part of the feelings exercise, so if your spouse is looking at his or her shoe or the ceiling, gently touch your spouse and ask him or her to look into the eyes that love them.

As couples practice this exercise, eye contact becomes more natural for them. Many couples state this was a significant shift for them in their overall communication. My wife Lisa has the biggest green eyes I have ever seen, and to look into them is to see her soul. For me to see her soul is what drives me crazy for her. As you practice this guideline to the feelings exercise, I hope that you experience this aspect of intimacy that transcends words.

Guideline Three: No Feedback. The last of the guidelines for the feelings exercise is just as important as the first two guidelines. As your husband or wife is sharing his or her feelings, there are to be no comments from you about the feelings being shared.

This is critical to keep the exercise safe for each spouse. When your spouse shares a feeling and you pump him or her for more information, your spouse is not going to feel safe and will be less likely to want to continue this very important exercise. Pumping for more information includes asking your spouse to tell you more or go into greater detail to further clarify his or her feelings.

Another violation of the "no feedback" guideline would be suggesting that your spouse "shouldn't feel that way." Just accept what is being said. Don't verbally interpret or comment on what is shared. Just say thank you and go ahead with *your* feeling word next.

The second aspect of the "no feedback" guideline is what I call the "seventy-two-hour" rule. Whatever is shared during the exercise *cannot* be discussed for seventy-two hours. In other words, suppose your wife shares a feeling of being "betrayed." Her first remembrance example was when she was six and her nine-year-old sister took her favorite Barbie doll and gave it to the dog. You are not to give feedback for at least seventy-two hours.

The reason for this is so you both have emotional safety. Intimacy, especially emotional intimacy, demands safety. If I am going to share my heart of hearts, I have to know above all things it is safe to do. You see, the feelings exercise isn't just about identifying and communicating feelings; it's day after day of experiencing each other as emotionally safe people.

Over time in your marriage, if the feelings your spouse shares get shoved back in his or her face when you are angry, your spouse will generalize that you are not safe and therefore will not want to share feelings with you. When you get defensive as your spouse shares with you, he or she will generalize that you are not an emotionally safe person to share with. If this is the routine way in which you respond to emotional intimacy, you both will feel unsafe sharing in your most primary relationship, your marriage.

As time goes by in a marriage that is emotionally unsafe, the spouse will choose not to be emotionally intimate. The need for emotional intimacy doesn't just go away for the spouse who doesn't share emotionally. He or she will seek another emotional outlet. It may be golf with the guys or lunch with the girls, but it won't be with each other. I feel truly sad for couples whose primary emotional intimacy is outside of their marriage.

Remember to follow the seventy-two-hour rule. If you do this, emotional safety will increase tremendously, and you will want to share your feelings with your spouse and enjoy the emotional intimacy that you both desire. I call it the abundant marriage, where you can be spirit, soul and body intimate for a lifetime.

Lisa and I have done this exercise for over seventeen years. After a three-month period, you can adjust the feeling structure, but I recommend that you stick to the structure and obtain the skill of the feelings exercise. I have experienced such safety with my wife, Lisa, in this area. Her acceptance of my feelings and heart without feedback has given me the opportunity to generalize that she is the safest person on the planet for my heart. My soul is saturated with my wife. This protects me from temptation and makes my life fun.

It's normal for us even throughout the day to stop each other and share what we are feeling at the moment or what we feel about a life event that day. I know I can call Lisa anytime and share positive or not-so-comfortable feelings with her, and she can do the same with me. For me, that is what emotional intimacy is about. It's the feeling of not being alone in this world but connected.

Daily Three: Praise and Nurturing

This is the last of the three daily exercises you have the opportunity to practice with your husband or wife over the next few months. This exercise addresses the need for nurturing and praise that every one of us has.

As parents we intuitively know our children need to hear "I love you, I'm proud of you, you're smart, great choice," and so on. I don't know where we get the notion that, as we become adults, we don't need nurturing. Yes, we need to be mature, but we are never without the need of nurturing.

You are the primary voice in your spouse's life. A silent voice is the cruelest thing you can give to your spouse. The spouse who hears neither bad nor good from the husband or wife to whom they committed their life grows hollow inside. Praise and nurturing is not something that all of us grew up with, especially as ACOSAs.

Praise and nurturing one another is an essential ingredient for a vibrant, ongoing, intimate relationship. While practicing praise and nurturing, you will get skilled and comfortable with the exercise of giving and receiving. For some husbands and wives, giving praise is difficult. For others, receiving or acknowledging praise is more difficult. Still for others, both aspects of giving and receiving praise are difficult.

Both the giving and receiving of praise is a skill. Again, skills can be learned by anyone. Anyone can praise and nurture a soul. As you practice the praise exercise daily, you and your spouse will experience the oil of intimacy drip into your soul and heal areas of dryness that you didn't even know existed.

When I counsel couples, I ask them when was the last time they received real praise, eye-to-eye and heart-to-heart, and not just the obligatory "Thanks, honey." They look at each other and shrug their shoulders. This is sad because this is the icing on the cake for me. When Lisa tells me something positive about myself almost every day, my soul leaps. I feel affirmed, and I can take on another day of life events. This is because I know in the deepest area of my heart that at the end of even the worst day of my life, those big green eyes of hers are going to look right into my heart and she's going to say something nice.

Now I ask you, how hard do you think it is to be around someone who affirms you at least daily? Not hard at all. We all love being around people who think that we're special or praiseworthy. It is even greater when that person is your spouse.

Imagine if you were going to take a very long journey, and you could choose between three spouses to travel with you. Spouse number one is critical most of the time. In your spouse's estimation, you don't know enough, you don't do things right, and you can't make him or her happy no matter what you do. I call this hell on Earth.

The second spouse is silent most of the time. He or she doesn't praise or compliment you, or really give you much of an opinion at all. Your spouse's gifts are all locked up in fear, and he or she feels too inferior to be a helpmate so you get to do it all spiritually, emotionally, sexually and financially. This is what I call purgatory on Earth; it isn't hell because at least you are in control, but it sure is lonely.

The last spouse knows how to compliment your qualities. He or she can stop on even the busiest day to offer a kind word and has learned the discipline of seeing the good in you. I call this heaven on Earth.

So which spouse would you pick, spouse #1, spouse #2 or spouse #3? I am sure most of us would like to be stuck with spouse #3 for a journey of forty or fifty years together if we had a chance to start all over again.

The great news is that you do get to start all over again. The other news is that *you* get to choose to be spouse #3 to your husband or wife, too. Isn't it great that you can choose to be spouse #3 by bringing praise and nurturing to your spouse?

Do you remember the principle of sowing and reaping we talked about earlier? If you sow praise in time, the harvest of nurturing and praise will come back to you.

The specifics of this exercise are very similar to the feelings exercise. First, you both individually think of two things that you love, appreciate or value about the other person.

The praises can apply to something your spouse did during the day, or simply a general appreciation for your spouse. When you both have two praises for each other, you can begin this exercise.

Let's suppose the husband starts first. Remember that the guideline of maintaining eye contact applies here as well. The husband looks into his wife's eyes and states, "I really appreciate that you are such a thrifty person, like the way you saved us money on checking into the mortgage insurance today."

Then the wife would continue to look at her husband until she accepted and let it into her heart. I purposely said "heart" and not "head." This is not a cognitive exercise but a heart exercise. After the wife has let the praise into her heart, she says, "Thank you."

The "thank you" is an important part of the exercise. This is when the recipient has received the praise in his or her heart. I used the word "received" because at first you may not agree with your spouse's praise due to lack of skill or feelings of inferiority, yet you acknowledge that you let the praise into your heart.

At this time the wife would give her husband his praise. When he lets it into his heart, he then says, "Thank you." Then he gives his wife a second praise, and she gives him a second praise with the follow-up words, "Thank you."

For example, I will use the following praises and appreciations that Trent and Natalie offer to each other. In our example, Trent will go first.

Trent:	*I really appreciate the extra effort you made today in completing the decorating project.*
Natalie:	*Thank you.*
Natalie:	*What I really love about you is that you are sincere about working on our marriage.*
Trent:	*Thank you.*
Trent:	*I love the way you laugh, it brings me such happiness to hear your laughter.*
Natalie:	*Thank you.*
Natalie:	*I appreciate you making time for me at lunch today.*
Trent:	*Thank you.*

This is how the praise and nurturing exercise sounds. It may look simple, but for some it is difficult work. This exercise is sweet. When it is combined with the other two daily exercises, it can make a profound shift in your intimacy. I am enjoying a lifestyle of both giving and receiving praise, and it has been great. Take the time to process this exercise together.

✳ ✳ ✳

I know these exercises will take time and work. The work part gets easier after ten days or so. The time part is going to be most important. As you and your husband or wife embark on improving or maintaining your intimacy, you will need to set a time to practice these exercises.

Some couples do all three daily exercises at the same time to make it easier. All three exercises, when you get to a level of skill, can take as little as ten to fifteen minutes each day. This is a small amount of time to develop a vibrant, love-giving, intimate marriage.

I would also suggest that you make yourselves accountable to a safe couple. The added accountability can add so much more motivation to make it through the next few months successfully.

This accountability can be as simple as a telephone call to check in daily, or just a one-time-a-month check-in meeting or lunch with this person. This person isn't supposed to give feedback or therapy. He or she is just hearing your progress on the three daily exercises: to pray, feel and praise together.

This was a lot of important information, so I want to review it briefly and follow up with an illustration of the whole process.

1. Pray daily with your spouse
2. Do two feelings exercises, following the guidelines
   a. no example about each other
   b. maintain eye contact
   c. no feedback
3. Do two praises daily with eye contact and follow up with a thank you

An example of a couple actually doing all three exercises is helpful for some couples to sense exactly what to expect. Let's look at what David and Ellen might say during the exercises.

Daily One: Prayer

David: God, I thank you for a great day and for being with Ellen, the children and me. Thanks for the commission you gave me today in my job and for helping Ellen during her day. I love you, thanks for everything.

Ellen: I, too, want to thank you God. You have been so good to

David and me. Thank you so much for providing all that we need and so much more. You are an awesome God. Thanks for little Tony's progress in school and for Darla's new friend Jennifer. We love you, thanks again.

Daily Two: Feelings

David: I feel enthusiastic when I close a deal like I did today at the office.

I first remember feeling enthusiastic when dad would wake me up early on Saturdays when I was about six years old just to say we were going fishing.

Ellen: I feel drained after being stuck in traffic twice today.

I first remember feeling drained when I was nine after being out in the snow until we were wet and cold from making snow angels.

David: I feel safe when I come home from work, and I know the phone finally isn't for me. I first remember feeling safe when I was ten years old in a football league, and I got to wear a real helmet and pads.

Ellen: I feel appreciated when Tony hugged me today and said, "You're the greatest mom." I first remember feeling appreciated when my mom made such a big deal to my dad that I cleaned my room without being told. I think I was about seven.

Daily Three: Praise and Nurturing

David: I really appreciate you being so patient with Darla's piano lessons every night.

Ellen: Thank you.

Ellen: I really appreciate you coming home thirty minutes early today and taking time to clean up the kitchen with me.

David: Thank you.

David: I love that you stay so attractive. Even in jeans and a T-shirt you are still so beautiful.

Ellen: Thank you.

Ellen: I love the fact that you just trust my judgment in different areas of our relationship.

David: Thank you.

And that's it—the three dailies! I hope you allow this structure to build the many skills that can enhance your marriage. You decide the skills you have. If you have great intimacy skills in your marriage, then your children can learn. As an ACOSA, you can experience a level of intimacy you have always wanted.

11

A Special Note for Mom

Most women reading this book will most likely have their dad as the sex addict. Some will have their mom as the sex addict. Either way, as a woman you have been impacted by sexual addiction. In my research and clinical practice, I have observed that quite a few daughters of sexual addicts end up marrying sexual addicts.

If you are reading this chapter and your husband is a sex addict, this will give you some things to actively think about. If you are the mom and you are the addict, some of these principles will apply to you as well.

It's Not All You

First, if your husband is the sex addict, there isn't anything you could have done to prevent his addiction. He was an addict as a teen, and you did not create this. There was no amount of your sex that would have made it go away. The addict is connected to objects, not people. If your husband is an addict, I would recommend you read *The Final Freedom* and *Sex, Men and God* to better understand the neuropathway conditioning of sex addicts.

Having said this, sex addiction does have a direct, measurable impact on the spouse of a sex addict. In my book *Partners: Healing from His Addiction,* we have several statistics about the impact of sexual addiction on the spouse of a sex addict. The most common impacts on a spouse are lower self-esteem, depression, overeating and control issues.

If you had some of these issues prior to marriage, they have probably gotten worse during the marriage. If you were a relatively healthy person prior to marriage, you would also have been impacted. And you were impacted by the addiction even if you didn't know it existed. The lack of connection and support from your husband, his selfishness, his sexual issues and what you learned about his addiction along the way helped guide your life.

Women in general are very protective about their mothering. Every woman not only wants to be a great mother, but she wants to be perfect. She wants her children to be great people. She works hard day in and day out. I honor all of what you have done and will do, yet no mother is perfect. All mothers are human, and humans are flawed but loved.

If we can push aside the normal mother's denial of mothering, we can have some honest conversations. Children, whether they're in their teens or their fifties, desire honesty, not the image of "Everything was okay" or "I did the best I could."

In our research and as you have observed throughout this book, ACOSAs often have mother issues as well as father issues. Many of these issues have to do with honesty, protection, sexual silence or negative sexual information.

Your husband's addiction, your addiction or the impact of his addiction *did* have an impact on the children. That is a fact. You may not like it or want to hear it, but it is true. You can't relive this part of their experiences and redo the parenting.

The pain of addiction was set in motion for the children on your watch—but it was not your fault. What your children choose to do with their pain is their choice. If they decide to get help and not be addicted or codependent, good for them, and if they choose the path of addiction, codependency and projecting a false self, this is also their choice.

You did not make their choices about how to handle the pain. The pain you want to look at is about what to do now. I know you tried; I know you love your children; I know you want what is best for them, so keep reading.

The Sick System

Your children not only were exposed to the sexual addiction, but the system to deal with the addiction. Children learn how systems work by watching their parents. For example, if Dad yells and screams to control Mom, children see it and will duplicate the system during adolescence .

If they see Dad controls Mom by money, the children learn several things. Women can be bought; money is more important than integrity; women can't take care of themselves financially; they need a man. Sons and daughters both see these roles and are likely to mimic these roles unless they get more information.

The system to cope with addiction is sick. You can't control an addiction. Yet when you're living in insanity, you want to get some control just to stop the emotional bleeding.

Denial and rationalizations are a huge problem in an addictive family. In the *Partners* book, I list a page of rationalizations. "Men are that way," "Boys will be boys," "At least he doesn't drink," "He doesn't hit me," "At least he holds a job." The rationalizations are endless.

The denial that it is just not happening is damaging to everyone. The addict is in denial to protect his or her behavior. The children wonder why Mom is in denial. Why can't she see everyone's unhappy? Why can't she see the insanity? Why won't she protect us? These are the experiences of children's hearts.

Dependency is absolutely a system sickness. Most women want to believe they stayed at home for the children. In my experience that is usually denial. The real reason most women stay home is financial. The second reason women stay with a sexually addicted husband is their own emotional dependence or fear of being alone.

Most women stay for the money. The dad knows this; the children know this; Mom is the only one in denial. This is an example of a system sickness. Dad denies his addiction, Mom denies her financial dependency and unwillingness to get a job, and voilà, you have a sick system. Actually, this particular system is the most common I see among addicts who don't have a need to get better.

I think you get the idea of what a sick system is. Often as a mom you are a part of that system. It is important for you to see the systems you cocreated when you chose to stay in an active sexual addict's household.

Your Healing Path

If you are a sex addict or the spouse of a sex addict, you deserve to heal. The best gift you can give to your children is a healthy, honest mother. Children can respect honesty even if they don't agree. It's dishonesty that confuses them and isolates them from you.

First, before you try fixing everyone in the family, start with you. Most sex addicts come to my office after their spouse gets healthier. For hundreds of women, the whole system changed, including the addict, once the women started getting healthier. It doesn't happen 100 percent of the time, but it works most of the time.

As the spouse starts putting up boundaries, getting her self-esteem built up or gets a job, things change. So start with you. I highly recommend the books *Partners: Healing from His Addiction* and *Partners Recovery Guide: 100 Empowering Exercises* and the video *Now That I Know, What Should I Do?* These two books and video are like therapy in a box. I know what it is like to grow up with a sexually addicted parent. I know the insanity firsthand. I also have worked with partners of sex addicts for eighteen years. These books are critical for your own recovery.

Second, get into a support group for partners of sex addicts. I know there are not many Partners, COSA, or S-Anon groups around. You can call our office or go to the Web site to see if there is one in your area.

If there isn't one in your area, we have several teleconference groups run by therapists to help you start making progress. Remember, you have to get strong first. Many addicts actively destroy their spouse's worth so they can control her. That is what you have to focus on before you attack the addiction or try to save your children.

If you feel you need counseling, get it as soon as possible. Find someone who understands sex addiction, sexual anorexia, partner issues and the family issues of sex addiction.

Once you feel strong enough, you can confront the addiction. Don't share this with your children. I find women want to tell the children to motivate the addict. That is not the best idea, and I would recommend you talk to a therapist before disclosing this to a child.

If the addict chooses help, support this and measure progress through a polygraph test to verify that the addiction is in remission. Remember, sex addicts can lie about their addiction and their recovery, so measure this.

If he doesn't want help, then you really have to decide why you are staying. You will need a huge dose of self-honesty, a support group and probably therapy. If you know your own truth, you will be okay. I had a woman tell me, "I'm staying for the country club and the lifestyle whether he changes or not." She was honest and wasn't playing any games with herself.

If your boundaries include in-house separation or physical separation, consult a therapist to make sure the goals of separation are clear. If you need legal counsel, see a local attorney regarding separation in your state.

I would also recommend that you re-read the Healing Path chapter and apply those exercises to your own healing. After this, you might be in a place to start addressing these issues with the children.

Inform Not Impose

Most mothers want what is best for their children. Many of you reading this book will have adult children. Adults don't always want what is best for themselves. Some people choose addiction over reality. Your children will make healthy and unhealthy choices; that's a part of being human.

They do have pain, and you need to honor that it's their pain and their choices. They might have already duplicated some of the sick systems that were present earlier in their life. It's hard to say each system is different, and each child is different. In my family I am the only one who chose a different path.

First, accept that as adults they have to choose their own path. You can't shame or humiliate them, get angry or try to be controlling. If you play any games, you are in trouble. I know you don't want to have them make the same mistakes. Parents have had that wish for thousands of years.

If your husband is in recovery, and he wants to disclose to the children with you, that would be the best situation. If he is in denial, you will still have to be very clear on what the real reason is for involving the children. Again, consult a professional if this is your situation.

If the children know about the addiction, or if they are struggling with their own addiction, then give them information. You walk a fine line as a mother. You want to stay on the informing side of things. You don't want to be imposing your new world view on your children. You can share where you are and what you are learning, but do it in an honest way, not a confronting way.

If your children want information about healing from the effects of being an ACOSA, or if they know about the addiction, you can send them each a copy of this book; it is designed for them.

Be Honest

By far the hardest part of being a mom is being imperfect. Because you are human, you made mistakes. Some mistakes were poor beliefs you held onto, some were behaviors you did and some were things you didn't know you should do. At some point in your healing you need to be honest.

Children, even adult children, can be forgiving of an honest heart. Regardless of what your beliefs or behaviors were, you can ask forgiveness. It's a mature thing to be able to acknowledge your weaknesses to your children. Remember, we are flawed but loved.

Your children don't expect perfection; they do have an expectation of honesty. If you were part of creating a survival system based on denials, rationalizations, dependency or control, be honest about your part. Don't involve the addict's behavior; you made choices along the way as well. Be honest about your choices. Then you can move forward in an honest relationship.

If you are a sexually addicted mother, this trip to honesty will be significantly harder. Your possible emotional, spiritual and moral abandonment are harder to break denial about. Your preference for being sexual rather than being present as a mom is difficult to accept about yourself.

If you are a sexually addicted mom, seriously consider support and therapy before trying to mend things with your children. The last thing they need is another empty promise on how things will be better. I recommend the books *She Has a Secret* and *Secret Solutions Workbook*. You deserve a life of recovery first. I guarantee that your children would appreciate your recovery far and above an empty promise.

Being a mom is tough. Being an honest, human, flawed mom makes it a little easier. Forgive yourself of any shortcomings and move forward with your children. Children have survived wars, famines, diseases and all kinds of addictions. They can survive their parent's addiction, their spouse's reactions and their cocreated systems.

Children are resilient. I am living poof that an ACOSA who was abandoned, abused, neglected and addicted can make choices to heal. There is always hope. Moms are great at providing hope. Remember to inform, not impose, be honest, and above all try to enjoy your children and grandchildren. Connect your heart to them; they still need your smile, so give it freely.

12

Professional Helpers

In addition to the vital attendance and involvement in a Twelve Step program, many ACOSAs benefit greatly from professional therapy. Does the idea of therapy frighten you? A general discussion of the types of therapy and treatment settings available might help you decide if therapy is for you.

Like the medical or financial fields, the mental-health field has various levels of professionally trained people. These professionals have a wide variety of philosophies and training perspectives, and they can meet the different needs of ACOSAs.

Let's review some of the various options for professional helpers.

Psychiatrist

Psychiatrists are medical doctors. They attend several years of medical school, and they are trained to look at biological reasons for problems with human beings. They are trained in medications that influence the chemistry of the brain. This professional can be a valuable help or support to ACOSAs who have been previously diagnosed with depression, manic depression, bipolar disease or other problems that require the supervision of a medical doctor. He or she can prescribe medications you might need to feel better, such as antidepressants.

If the psychiatrist has had addiction training, or has had exposure to workshops dealing with sexual addiction and its ramifications on family members, he or she may be of some help to you as you work on your issues.

Psychologist

A psychologist is quite different from a psychiatrist, although they are often confused with each other. Psychologists have a Ph.D., Ed.D. or Psy.D., not an M.D. like medical doctors. They have not attended and graduated from medical school. They are not licensed physicians. Therefore, they cannot prescribe medication. They spend their educational training looking at the cognitive, or thinking, aspects of the human being, such as Intelligence Quotient, reading and math levels, psychological testing, and the like. He or she is often trained to do individual, group and marital therapy.

A psychologist with a doctorate in psychology can be of great help to the ACOSA, especially if he or she has had experience working with sex addicts and their families. A psychologist can also be of help to an ACOSA who is experiencing any psychological disorder, such as depression, suicidal thoughts, or a compulsive eating, sleeping or alcohol disorder. Often these survival mechanisms respond well to treatment under the care of a trained and licensed psychologist.

Licensed Professional Counselor

The licensed professional counselor, or LPC, usually has either master's level training or Ph.D. level training with expertise in counseling or a related field, such as sociology or anthropology. He or she can acquire a counselor's license through taking certain counseling classes. A master's degree is the minimum required for the LPC in most states. The master's level professional may also have a degree in an area other than counseling, like an M.Ed. (master's in education) and take ten or fifteen classes in counseling during or after his or her graduate degree program, to acquire a professional license from the state he or she practices in. This is something to note in your initial interview with a licensed professional counselor. You can ask exactly what his or her background is because some licenses may not require a degree in counseling in some states. This can be important for ACOSAs to know when they are seeking help for their own issues or for the issues regarding their family, marriage or children.

The master's level LPC, much like a psychologist, can be a great resource for ACOSAs who deal with family and individual problems. An LPC is usually able to identify and deal with depression, obsessive/compulsive disorders, addictive disorders, codependency and other issues. LPCs, like psychiatrists and psychologists, have ongoing training and, in most states, will have a more reasonable fee structure for those seeking counseling. In finding a licensed professional counselor, ask how many years he or she has been practicing, and review the Questions to Ask section at the end of this chapter to determine the counselor's experience with sexual addiction treatment or children of sexual addict's experience.

Social Worker

Social workers will have either a bachelor's or a master's level education. They may have several levels of certification, which can differ from state to state. They may be a certified social worker (CSW) or a master's level social worker (MSSW), depending on their experience. Their training is mostly from a social perspective. Seeing issues from a social perspective is beneficial and can be helpful, but unless specific training is given to the social worker in the field of addictions, there may be limits as to how helpful they can be.

However, if there is a need for social services for the family—for example, in finding places for residential treatment—a social workers are usually be quite resourceful. In some states, social workers are much like licensed professional counselors, as they provide individual, group or family therapy. In other states and situations, they may do social histories and things of that nature. In finding social workers, you will need to find out what educational training and experience they have had. You may find that this will be a very beneficial relationship to you. Again, refer to the Questions to Ask section at the end of this chapter for further information.

Pastoral Counselor

Pastoral counselors have professional degrees in counseling from an accredited seminary or institution. They may have a doctoral level education (Ph.D.), or they may have master's level education. Pastors of local congregations would be included in this category. Although many pastors have at least a bachelor's level education, some may have no formal education at all. Such counselors can be significantly helpful to those who have strong church, Christian or religious backgrounds. Pastoral counselors can be very helpful in your recovery because the development of spirituality is a significant part of recovery for the whole person.

The strengths of a pastoral counselor would include his spiritual training, coupled with professional experience and professional training in the fields of addictions, or counseling and psychological training. With such training, a pastoral counselor could be of benefit.

Some possible weaknesses of the pastoral counselor might be a lack of training or skill in some areas. The pastor who has had no training in counseling may be of brief support to the ACOSA, but might not be as beneficial in resolving personal issues or identifying other psychological problems.

The pastoral counselor, like all other professionals discussed, should be asked the appropriate questions from the Questions to Ask section. This is very important. Often, an understanding of addictions and sexual issues can influence how therapeutic the pastoral counselor can be to you.

Christian Counselor

Christian counseling is another form of counseling that is now readily available in larger cities, as well in some smaller communities. Christian counseling is not exactly the same as pastoral counseling. Many Christian counselors do not hold a position as a pastor, nor will they have professional pastoral counselor education training.

A Christian counselor is often professionally trained in the theory of counseling, psychology and human development. These counselors can be master's or doctoral level trained professionals, but the training they receive can vary widely. It is wise to check the Christian counselor's training prior to having any therapeutic relationship.

There is a specific benefit in having Christian counselors for those who embrace the Christian faith. They can be a great source of help, especially if they are able to integrate biblical truths and biblical understanding into the healing process. They can be very supportive and encouraging to the personal development of the ACOSA, and can also facilitate growth for the whole family. Again, ask questions relating to training and expertise in the area of sex addiction. Just because they are Christian does not guarantee they understand or successfully treat issues related to being an ACOSA.

Certified Alcohol and Drug Addiction Counselor or Licensed Chemical Dependency Counselor

CADACs and LCDCs are available in most areas, although their designations may differ from state to state. These are counselors with a variety of training backgrounds. They may have a Ph.D., a master's or bachelor's degree, or may have had no formal education whatsoever. Again, the training of an individual counselor is very significant. This cannot be stressed more than in the field of alcohol and drug addictions.

In some states, individuals recovering from alcoholism or drug addiction who want to enter the helping profession find that such certification is the easiest way into this field. They do have a valid experience and understanding of the addiction process, as well as understanding of the recovery process. However, caution must be used in that recovering people often have multiple addiction problems. This is something to be noted when interviewing addiction counselors.

In addition, it is important to ask how they have integrated the Twelve Step philosophy into their own lives. My personal opinion is that unless a counselor has completed at least a fourth and fifth step and has begun making amends, his or her perceptions might still be clouded by guilt and shame, and the counselor might not be able to facilitate the growth you need in your life.

Addiction counselors do have some strengths, however. They are often trained in family systems theory. They are familiar with the dynamics of addiction and usually come from a Twelve Step perspective. Often these counselors can be found working in alcohol and drug addiction treatment centers. Sometimes they share an office with a psychiatrist, psychologist or master's level counselor. They are often supervised in their work by a degreed professional.

You can ask if their caseload is being supervised, and by whom, and what that supervision process is. This is important because some supervisors, due to time constraints, will not review each case thoroughly. Another benefit to an addiction counselor is that he or she would be aware of recovery groups in the area and the importance of these support groups.

Marriage and Family Counselor

Marriage and family counselors can also have a variety of educational degrees. They may have a Ph.D. or a master's degree in marriage and family counseling. For ACOSAs, this may or may not be helpful, depending on the situation. If you are in a marriage or a committed relationship, such a counselor can be very beneficial.

Marriage and family counselors come from a family systems approach, taking into consideration the needs of the entire family, not just the needs of one person. Also, they will be highly attuned to how each family member processes problems and how the family members interact with each other.

For example, in some addictive systems the addict is the one who is perceived as needing help, the wife is the one who is strong and "helps" the addict, while the children are her supporters and cheerleaders in helping Dad. From a systems approach, a counselor might look at this situation and say, "Dad needs to be sick, so that Mom can be a helper." Mom needs to give up the helper role and establish her own identity and boundaries, so if Dad recovers, the family doesn't need somebody else to be sick.

The marriage and family counselor will be highly astute in these matters and can be beneficial to the ACOSA, as well as to the family as a whole. Refer to the Questions to Ask section to determine what training and experience this counselor has in addictions in general, and in sexual addiction specifically, as well as in recovery from being an ACOSA.

Telephone Counseling

The number of professionals who treat ACOSAs and sex addiction with a great deal of success can be limited even in a larger metropolitan area. Heart to Heart Counseling Centers has established telephone counseling for the ACOSA, the sex addict, the partner of a sex addict and for couples.

This form of counseling is especially helpful for those who travel quite a bit because they can call in for their appointment from anywhere and speak to the same counselor every week. Telephone counseling is also helpful to those who feel that their confidentiality is of utmost importance. We counsel many physicians, lawyers, ministers, entrepreneurs and students who don't want to run into their addiction counselor at the grocery store. They also don't have to walk into their counselor's office where they may be seen by someone they know. Some like it because they don't have to locate a baby-sitter to set up an appointment.

For whatever reason, ACOSAs have found help using the phone for counseling. It has been very successful for their recovery process. Working with a counselor who understands and is trained in working with adult children can expedite your recovery.

Three Day Intensives

At Heart to Heart Counseling Center, we have set up Three Day Intensives for ACOSAs. These intensives have been greatly successful in addressing the core issues that impact ACOSAs. Your therapist is a specialist in sex addiction, partners of sexual addicts, and the issues that impact you as an ACOSA. If you have an interest in attending a Three Day Intensive in Colorado Springs, call our office at 719-278-3708.

The choice of an appropriate treatment setting is also significant for the ACOSA. Treatment settings will vary considerably depending upon your location. Rural areas might present limited choices.

Larger metropolitan areas will offer most types of treatment settings. In addition to private facilities, you can also check into what community and state resources are available. Again, it will depend on your particular history and needs.

You are worth receiving professional help during your recovery process. Utilize this process to expedite your healing. Remember that now you have to meet *your* needs. I encourage you to examine your needs and do what is necessary for you to have the highest quality of life.

It is very appropriate to interview the professional you are considering as your therapist. Each person has a different history and could have possible conflicts with certain professionals due to their past experiences. Also, the many professionals discussed here represent a sort of continuum of care. At one point in recovery you might find one type of professional more helpful than another. Many practices include several types of therapists and are able to treat ACOSAs from a multidisciplinary view. In interviewing a potential therapist, consider the following list of questions.

Questions to Ask

❑ Do you have experience working with sexual addiction?

❑ Do you have experience working with adult children of sexual addiction or adult children of alcoholism?

❑ How many sex addicts have you seen in the last two months?

❑ Do you have training to do therapy with people with addictions? (state or board certification)

❑ Are you a recovering person working a Twelve Step program?

❑ What books have you read on sexual addiction?

❑ Do you have specific training to deal with (if these issues apply to you) rape victims, survivors of child sexual abuse, incest or other trauma?

13

The Twelve Steps

Now we enter into the recovery program known as the Twelve Steps. The original Twelve Steps were written many years ago for Alcoholics Anonymous. A group of alcoholics, after some period of sobriety, decided to write down the principles and the steps they took to maintain their sobriety and live a healthier life. These principles and steps have been used throughout the world to help millions of people with addictions such as narcotics abuse, overeating, emotional problems, codependency, sexual addiction and now for ACOSAs.

The Twelve Steps of Alcoholics Anonymous
Adapted for Adult Children of Sexual Addicts

1. We admitted we were powerless over our parent's sexual addiction and that our lives had become unmanageable.
2. We came to believe that a power greater than ourselves could restore us to sanity.
3. We made a decision to turn our wills and our lives over to the care of God, as we understood God.
4. We made a searching and fearless moral inventory of ourselves.
5. We admitted to God, to ourselves and to another human being the exact nature of our wrongs.
6. We were entirely ready to have God remove all these defects of character.
7. We humbly asked God to remove our shortcomings.
8. We made a list of all persons we had harmed and became willing to make amends to them all.
9. We made direct amends to such people wherever possible, except when to do so would injure them or others.
10. We continued to take personal inventory, and when we were wrong, promptly admitted it.
11. We sought through prayer and meditation to improve our conscious contact with God as we understood God, praying only for knowledge of God's will for us and the power to carry that out.
12. Having had a spiritual awakening as the result of these steps, we tried to carry this message to others and to practice these principles in all our day-to-day living.

Note: The Twelve Steps are reprinted and adapted with permission of Alcoholics Anonymous World Services, Inc. Permission to reprint and adapt the Twelve Steps does not mean that AA has reviewed or approved the content of this publication, nor that AA agrees with the views expressed herein. AA is a program of recovery from alcoholism. Use of the Twelve Steps in connection with programs and activities that are patterned after AA, but that address other problems, does not imply otherwise.

An Interpretation of the Twelve Steps for Adult Children of Sexual Addicts

What I will attempt to do in the following pages is explain the principles and concepts of the Twelve Steps as they are used for recovery from your parent's sexual addiction so you can implement them in your personal recovery. My comments here should not be construed as representing any particular Twelve Step fellowship. They are my own interpretation of the steps from my own experience, as well as from years of clinical experience helping ACOSAs recover by using the Twelve Step process.

Step One: We admitted we were powerless over our parent's sexual addiction and that our lives had become unmanageable.

We. I am so glad that the first word in the first step is "we." I would hate to think I was the only person who ever went through this. Being a child of a sexual addict is an international problem. "We" means that we have similar experiences, and we are alike. We grew up in the same family thousands of miles apart. We had the same kind of parents, abuses and neglects. "We" is a comforting word in this step. You can see that you are not alone and don't have to be alone. You can get better if you decide to get together. "We" is an encouraging word and is also essential. Without each other, we often fail to fully recover from the effects of our parent's sexual addiction.

Admitted. This is a difficult word. Many of us have had situations in our childhood for which we have had to admit. Maybe we stole something or something happened to us, and we had to admit what we did. Do you remember those feelings of dread before you admitted something? Then you went ahead and admitted it. You told what you did or what happened to you. After you admitted it, you felt less heavy or burdened, as if you could now move on. Admitting is one of the hardest things for ACOSAs to do in their recovery. Admitting is a very important aspect of recovery, and only those who admit to the sexual addiction of their parents and the pain it caused them can move forward in recovery and life.

We Were Powerless. Again, I'm glad that there is a "we" in there and that I'm not the only one who is powerless. When we talk about power, we talk about control, authority, strength or force that gives us the ability to be over someone else. But that is not what this word means. This word is "powerless," and as we know, the suffix "less" means without—such as jobless. This is a tough reality for every ACOSA. We are without any strength, power, control or force to influence the impact of our parent's sexual addiction. We are powerless over the reality that our parent(s) are sexual addicts. This is why we need each other and a recovery program. Sometimes that is why we need therapy. We are powerless.

Over Our Parent's Sexual Addiction. I know by the word "our" that others might understand what I have been through. We all need our parents. It is not a human want but a need to be connected to those who birthed us. The sex addiction of our parent(s) limits or annihilates the connection between them and us.

They chose sex over us. For whatever reason—abuse, neglect, chemical reinforcement, their family of origin—they still took their pain and chose to act out sexually. They not only disregarded the well-being of themselves and their spouse, but also their children.

They had some awareness there might be consequences, and they were willing to risk us to have their pleasure. Their defilement became our upbringing. They are addicts; we have to accept that cold fact in Step One. That fact may have serious repercussions for us, but accepting their sexual addiction is critical.

And That Our Lives. Our lives can be many things. It can be our physical, emotional, intellectual, spiritual, sexual and relational life. If you look at all the parts of our lives, they still wouldn't equal the totality of our lives. Our lives are the very core of us. It is the inner part of us that identifies us as being separate from another person. This is what has been affected by our parent's sexual addiction. This is the part that feels disconnected, alone, confused and isolated when needs are not being met. It is this part of us that we are going to admit something very important about.

Had Become. These two words indicate to me that this has taken a while. It means that it took time, energy, process and choices. It didn't just happen. It took a while, and then eventually, it was made. Your awareness of your parent's sexual addiction probably came over time. Your life didn't become overwhelming or devastated instantly, but over a period of time.

Unmanageable. When we think about manageable, we think about things being in order or serene. We can tell when we walk into a store whether the store is manageable or unmanageable. This word means unorganized and chaotic. If someone came from the outside and saw this, they would say "What a mess!" Sometimes this is the way we feel, and our feelings can be valid. Our lives in many of the areas we have talked about have become unmanageable, unconnected, uncontrollable and unpredictable. No matter how hard we have tried to make them look good or perfect, they don't and they are not. Our lives have been impacted in some ways by our parent's sexual addiction. Now, through Step One, if we can admit this unmanageability, we have a strong hope of recovery.

I encourage everyone to take Step One seriously because it is the foundation of the Twelve Step program. It will cause you to have a good house of recovery to live in for the future.

Step Two: We came to believe that a power greater than ourselves could restore us to sanity.

We Came to Believe. Again, notice the step is written in the past tense. The original steps were written to share the process that the original members of AA went through in recovery. There was a process through which they came to believe.

It is really a simple process. You come to believe many things during your lifetime. For example, you came to believe there was a Santa Claus. Later you came to believe there wasn't a Santa Claus. As you grew older, you may have come to believe that a certain person liked you, and later realized they didn't like you. We come to believe certain religious and political positions. There is some consistency to this process throughout our lives. In this process, there is a definite point at which you understand or come to believe.

In Twelve Step groups, the process of coming to believe often happens as a result of exposure to other recovering people. You may not necessarily know the date or the hour when you did come to believe, but you know that you feel differently, and you begin to hope. This is so important in recovery because knowing that you have come to believe, or knowing you do believe, can save your life. Adult children of sex addicts can get down, feel hopeless or worthless, experience severe shame and guilt from past traumas or present circumstances, and resort to sad behaviors of destruction, isolation, sexual acting out and suicidal ideation. If you have come to believe, you have hope that God cares for you, loves you and accepts you.

That a Power. "A" is a common word. You use it every day. A cat, a dog, a book—and in every context in which it is used, it denotes one. If you were going to use a word to describe more than one, you would say "these," or another word that indicates plurality. This step is not written in the plural. It says "a" power greater than us. This is significant. Being an "a" here, you realize that there is one entity, one strength, one energy, one spirit, one power. It is significant that as you come to believe, you believe in one.

Greater Than Ourselves. This is one of the first areas that requires trust from the ACOSA. We now know there is one who is greater than ourselves. This is the best news we have in recovery; we don't have to figure this out alone. As you begin to trust this power, you begin to recover from the sick patterns, poor choices, and undesirable relationships or other aspects from your parent's sexual addiction.

In the original context of AA, this power greater than ourselves indicated that the power was greater than that first group of recovering alcoholics. This one single power was greater than a whole group. That's a lot of power. People in recovery frequently first recognize this power in the group, but in reality it is greater than the group. Even if you had a power greater than yourself, you may have had difficulty accessing the resources of that power and applying them to your life. In the program, you come to believe that this power has more ability to solve life's problems than you do individually. What a relief!

Could. "Could" is one of the most helpful, loving expressions in the Twelve Steps. Could this power have the ability, the resources, the energy and the intention of helping you along in the recovery process? It is now possible to begin to be restored. It is now possible to begin to be healthy, to have loving relationships with loving people, and to be loved and nurtured in a healthy way. It can be done, and this power can do it. It is the experience of many in recovery that, if given the freedom and the opportunity—in other words, when you quit trying to do it all on your own—this power will do for you what you have been unable or unwilling to do for yourself. All you have to do is ask.

Restore Us to Sanity. "Restore" means bringing back something. Frequently when you think of restoration, you think of restoring an automobile or an old house and making it look like new. The same is true of recovery from your parent's sexual addiction.

Adult children of sexual addicts have for so long been robbed of true spirituality, intimacy, trust and even their own reality. In a world that should have been safe, we were violated or let down again and again.

Insanity is natural when you live with a parent who is a sex addict. You may have difficulty applying the idea of insanity to yourself, but often your parent(s) having two lifestyles at the same time and living with the secret can make the people around them feel insane. You try again and again to do something to be loved, connected to or valued, but it doesn't work.

The behaviors themselves are insane, but the fact that you use them again and again, never stopping to realize that they're not working, qualifies you to be restored to sanity. It is possible for ACOSAs to be restored to sanity. Those already in recovery have experienced it. They are living proof that it is possible to make better choices, and we hope, as you read this, that you know it is possible for you. You may still feel crazy, but if you have gotten this far in your recovery, you have a good chance at finding sanity in all areas of your life.

Step Three: We made a decision to turn our wills and our lives over to the care of God, as we understood God.

We Made. "Made" is kind of like "became." It indicates a process that involves time and choices, but there is definitely a time when it is done. For example, when kids in school make an ashtray, or a meal in home economics, or a dress, there is a time when it is in the process of being made, and then it is completed. It is made. "Made" is something that is resolved to the point that you can say it is done.

A. Here again we come to that little word "a." It is one. What we are discussing in Step Three is a one-time event. Many people want to spread this step out, but as you move along in this process of working the steps, you will see why we only make this decision one time.

Decision. When you make a decision, you list the good and the bad, the pros and cons of a situation. In this step, you can make a list of what you have done with your life, and how you could deal with your life differently in the future. Such a list makes it easier to make the decision you are asked to make in Step Three. It is a decision.

Compare it to a traditional courtship and marriage. It is as if you had an engagement period in Step Two, during which you got to know your power greater than yourself and you began to get comfortable with the idea of having God in your life. Step Three is the marriage ceremony itself, where you make a commitment to share your life with God. You have a single ceremony that sets the stage for further development through the relationship. Step Three asks you to be willing to share your life with God. The decision is a one-time event, but it provides a means for further growth.

To Turn. Turning can be expressed in many ways. Someone said once that turning means "to flip over," kind of like a hot cake. The hot cake gets done on one side, and then you have to turn it over. That's a pretty simple definition of turn, but it is also pretty profound. If you flip over, you make a total change from the way you have been.

"Turn" is used on highways all over the world to indicate direction: Signs may indicate a left or right turn, or U-turn. When you make a U-turn, you turn around and go in the opposite direction. What you do in Step Three is definitely a U-turn! You turn away from your limited understanding of how life should be. You leave behind perceptions, experiences and ideas about things you thought you understood. You turn from them and gain a whole new perspective. This is an essential part of recovery. You are turning into something, or turning somewhere else, and it is amazing how far that turn can take you.

Our Wills. Again, this is plural, as the group stays and works together. In this group of safe people, who have turned their wills and lives over to God, you begin to see this decision as a possibility for yourself. But what is your will? The simplest definition of "will" is probably the ability to make the choices you do for your life. In the group, you will begin to turn over your choices to God. This can be an easy thing for some, but for others it can be a very hard thing to do, especially if one of the side effects of your parent's sexual addiction is you like control. It means you must turn your freedom over to God, try to understand God's perspective, and follow that perspective in your life. That is why Step Three is so powerful.

As I have mentioned before, in many recovery groups there is a phrase called "stinking thinking." Stinking thinking is the way an addict, alcoholic or an adult child thinks. This thinking doesn't work. The choices nonrecovering people make don't bring about positive results. There seems to be a certain self-destructiveness to their choices and behavior. Step Three cuts to the core of stinking thinking. It is the beginning of a new lifestyle.

Giving up our will is a safety valve for ACOSAs. In making decisions about relationships, we are now able to turn to God. When we
do, God will demonstrate new directions we can take and new
choices we can make. We will begin getting answers and be able to
make different choices in all areas of our lives. This is a freedom
that is only gained by letting go of our own wills, or choices.

And Our Lives Over. Our lives are the result of all our choices.
For each individual, life is the totality of all parts. When you turn it
all over—spiritually, emotionally, physically, socially, relationally,
financially and sexually—you give yourself to God. You begin to
trust God. You begin to believe that God will take care of you.

You may think this is frightening: "How can I trust God?!" But
look at what you have trusted in the past. You have trusted your own
ability to think, your own ability to make choices. You have taken
the advice of a few chosen people who have not necessarily acted in
your best interests.

Turning your will and life over is necessary. It is through this
trust experience with God that you begin to believe God loves you.
You begin once again to trust yourself. Eventually, you can even
regain your trust in healthy people. Step Three is an essential part of
working the steps. It is not a luxury. It is necessary for a healthy,
happy life. Working the steps is not always easy, and often you do
not understand why you must work them. The steps are often understood only after they have been completed. Then you realize the
beauty of this spiritual process and open yourself to further growth
and joy as you walk this road with others who are making the same
steps toward recovery.

To the Care of God. What do you think of when you hear the
word "care"? It is often expressed in terms of someone who loves
you, someone who demonstrates kindness toward you, someone
who is willing to get involved in your life, willing to get in there and
be patient with you and work with you and not condemn you in the
process, someone who can be nurturing. All these pictures of a loving parent or friend can represent care. Care is felt in the release of

energy from one person to another, usually through kind behaviors, like providing a listening ear or some other sign of concern.

How does this relate to God? What is the care of God? It is simply God's willingness to be involved in a nurturing, supportive, accepting way in your life. God is concerned for ACOSAs. God's concern for others in this world demonstrates that care. You can sometimes see it more clearly in the lives of others than you can in your own life. For some ACOSAs, the group is a manifestation of the care of God in their lives. It is possible for you, by looking at others in your support group, to connect with this issue in such a way that it radically changes your life. Something as simple as their support can be seen as the extension of God's care and concern.

Now we'll talk about God. The original writers of the Twelve Steps changed only one word from the initial version. In Step Two they changed the word "God" to "a Power greater than ourselves." That is the only change they made, and it was made for this reason: Those first alcoholics said that God was too scary for the recovering person in Step Two. Maybe the recovering person had too many hurts, too many problems with God, so the wording was changed to "a Power greater than ourselves" to give newcomers an engagement period and allow them to experience God through the group's care, nurturing and love. In this way they could come to believe in a caring God who could, and would, help them.

But who is God? Let me share my thoughts with you on this subject. Simply put, God is love. God is in authority or in control, especially for those who turn their lives and will over to him and switch the authority from themselves to God.

God has the ability to restore you. God is more powerful than you are alone, or as a group. God is one who gets actively involved in your life, who has more power and more success than you in dealing with the impact of your parent's sexual addiction. This God can and will help you as you work the Twelve Steps.

For many, this understanding of God will develop into a faith that is common in the American culture. It will enable us to enjoy the benefits of finding a community that shares the same faith. Some will not. It is a universal blessing of this program, however, that people will, if they are willing, come to a greater relationship with God.

The people who have turned their wills and lives over to the care of a God they understand—who have turned their choices over to God—often have more understanding of how God works and how God thinks. The group is a good resource, especially for those early in recovery. It is very important to realize, as it pertains to understanding God, that no single person is going to understand the totality of God, but the members of your support group can be helpful in this journey.

As We Understood God. One way to interpret this is to compare your understanding of God with the way you function in relationships with people, because we are talking about a relationship. When you first meet someone, your knowledge of this person is limited. Only through time, communication and commitment to a relationship do you really come to understand another person. The same is true of your relationship with God. Coming to understand God is a process that is available to any and all in recovery who are willing to turn their wills and lives over so they can experience a new life, freedom and happiness. The beauty of finding God in the Twelve Steps is that as you grow, your understanding of God grows, too.

Step Four: We made a searching and fearless moral inventory of ourselves.

We Made a Searching. Searching holds the possibility of fun, but for ACOSAs, searching can be extremely painful. When you search, you intend to find something. For example, when you lose your keys, you go searching with the intent of finding the keys. As you begin your search inventory, you are searching, you are scrutinizing, and you are seeking with intent to find something that is quite significant.

In this context, "searching" indicates that you will have to expend some energy. This is the beginning of what is often referred to in the program as "action steps." You now begin to take action on your own behalf. Note that this step is also in the past tense. As you begin your inventory, know that others have passed this way before and have survived and gotten better. You are not alone.

And Fearless. "Fearless" simply means without fear. This is the attitude with which you approach your moral inventory. Being fearless allows you to view your inventory objectively as you uncover the pain. You will be looking at what was done to you and what you have done to yourself and others.

Many of the experiences you will be looking at are extremely painful. For some ACOSAs, it will be things they would much rather forget, things they may think they only imagined. Fearlessness will lead you to look at your own part in the sick relationships you have been in as an adult and at the patterns that have been repeated over and over in your life. You need to look at these things with an attitude of courage and bravery. You can, because in Step Three you turned your will and life over to the care of a loving God.

Moral. "Moral" can be defined as right and wrong, categories of black and white, or good and bad. Something that is immoral violates your conscience. As you look at your life in Step Four, you will be looking for things that you've done that have violated your conscience. For example, as children, many of us had the experience of raiding the cookie jar. We knew we were not supposed to get a cookie. There might not be anything wrong with having a cookie, but we were told not to, so it became wrong. Yet we waited until our parents could not see and took a cookie anyway. It probably tasted good, but we may have felt bad afterward. We felt bad because we knew we did something wrong.

In Step Four, you will also be looking at how you were violated by others. Have you ever said to yourself, "If they really knew me, they wouldn't like me," or "If they knew I was sexually abused or raped, they wouldn't be my friend"? The shame and guilt you carry from the actions of other people toward you can be overwhelming. Step Four is designed to release you from that shame and guilt as you look at how your moral code has been violated by others.

It is wrong to believe that you are unworthy because of your past or the sexual addiction of your parent(s). In recovery, you come to know yourself and let others know you. Step Four is about coming to know yourself, being honest with yourself about what happened, taking into account how it affected your life, and where it leaves you today.

Inventory. In short, Step Four is an inventory. You will list everything that happened, even if it involved others and you were simply an innocent bystander—as in the case of the divorce of parents, or the death of a grandparent or other significant family member. Such an event may not have had anything to do with your morals, but it did affect you emotionally.

What are you to inventory in Step Four? You inventory your experiences because, as a human being, that is what you have on hand. You inventory your memory, for that is what you have been given to record your experiences. Many see this inventory as a life story. It is a process where you begin to see the truth of what you've done and what has been done to you. Some things will be negative; others will be positive. When a storekeeper takes inventory, he lists not only the things he wants to get rid of, but also the things he wants to keep. And he doesn't just make a mental note of it—he writes it down.

Step Four is a written assignment. You will need to have pen or pencil, paper, and a quiet place where you can be uninterrupted. Some just begin writing. Some organize their inventory by ages, such as zero to six years, seven to twelve years, and so on. Still others have done it by first listing all the traumatic events they can remember—things that were done to them or by them that violated their value system—and then writing how they felt at the time and how they now feel about those events. There is no right or wrong way to write an inventory. The important thing is just to do it. You will be face to face for perhaps the first time with the total reality of your life. It can be pretty overwhelming, so don't be afraid to let your sponsor or therapist know how you are feeling while writing your inventory. As you transfer your story to paper, you are also transferring the pain, guilt and shame. Writing an inventory can be a very positive transforming experience, and it is vital to your recovery from your parent's sexual addiction.

Of Ourselves. Once again, you can see this is plural. You can know that others have done this before. You can survive the pain of writing down your inventory. It is joyous to see others freed from their shame. As you see other members of your support group complete their inventories, you will begin to believe this release from shame can happen for you, too. You are reminded that only you can do this for yourself. Only you know your pain, the strength of your fears, your deepest secrets. Only you are qualified to write this inventory. Now is the time to decide for yourself who you are and who you want to be. There is great freedom in taking your focus off what is wrong with others and doing a searching and fearless moral inventory of yourself. You may not understand the value of this step until you have completed it, but it is well worth the pain and tears.

Step Five: We admitted to God, to ourselves and to another human being the exact nature of our wrongs.

We Admitted. Here you are again, looking at that word "admitted." You already know that it means to "fess up," or acknowledge what is already true. You may have already experienced the pain and joy of doing this, probably as a child or adolescent. Perhaps you put yourself in a situation you knew your parents would not approve of, or did something wrong, and knew you were going to have to tell them—because you knew they were going to find out anyway. Do you remember your feelings of guilt and shame, like you had let yourself and them down? Then you somehow got the courage to tell them what you had done. You admitted the truth—no matter the consequences. It felt better, finally, to let the secret out.

The same is true in Step Five. You admit all that you have written in Step Four. You let out all those secrets and finally feel that clean joy that comes from truly being totally known.

To God. God might be the easiest person to tell, or the hardest, depending on your relationship with him. If you feel God has let you down before, admitting what has been wrong in your life can be particularly difficult. Fortunately, God is forgiving of all that you have done, and he is willing to restore any lost part of yourself. As one wise person in recovery stated, "It's okay to tell God. God already knows it all anyway and is just waiting for us to be honest about it, too."

To Ourselves. Admitting your past secrets to yourself often takes place as you write Step Four, if you are truly fearless and thorough when writing it. Admitting your powerlessness, your need to be restored to sanity, your profound amazement at your poor choices and your sincere sense of having failed yourself is probably the most humbling experience you will have with regard to your sense of who you are.

It is at this point, though, that the recovery of your true self is able to take an upward turn, without the overwhelming sense of shame or guilt that has been so closely bound to you in the past. You are now able to begin a more shame-free life, which empowers you to experience the next and most essential part of this step: being able to reveal yourself to another human being.

And to Another Human Being. "What? I have to tell all this stuff to somebody else, face to face?" Yes, telling your story to another human being is the most crucial part of your recovery. In writing Step Four, you have taken your total history of shame, hurt, abandonment, abuse, poor choices and acting out, and poured it consciously into one place. Your Step Four may have even brought to your awareness some things you have been suppressing for years, and now all of these memories are in one place. If all this pain is kept inside you, and is not shared with another human being, you may talk yourself into believing once again that you are unlovable or unacceptable with such a painful, messy past. You could use this negative information and history for condemnation instead of healing. That is why we must tell another person. We must realize that we are loved and accepted, even though we have been places and experienced things of which we are not proud. Remember, we as humans are flawed but loved.

In Step Five you experience spiritually, emotionally and often physically a cleansing or a lightening of your load. As you share who you have been and what you have experienced with another trusted person, you are reassured that nothing you have done makes you unlovable. Now someone knows the whole truth and still loves you. It is remarkable!

A note of caution: When you choose someone to hear your Step Five, it is important to pick the least condemning, most loving and accepting person you know. You might choose a therapist, sponsor or spiritual person you trust. Choose someone who understands that you are digging into your past in order to make your present and future better—someone who will not shame you for your past. This person can be a member of your support group. This choice is yours. Make it in your best interest.

The Exact Nature of Our Wrongs. The fact that this part of the step is so specific will help two kinds of people: those who say "I can't be specific so I'll never really feel loved," and those who believe they can own everybody else's wrongs and avoid looking at their own choices. The first person needs to be specific in sharing his or her story, because the shame they experience about the past is tied to specific episodes. We must talk about those specific episodes to relieve the shame associated with them. The second person needs to acknowledge his or her own shortcomings and "clean their own side of the street"—not anyone else's—so they too can be freed from their own shame.

It's a recognized fact that you can't free anyone else from his or her shame. Each person has to work his or her own program of recovery in order to have the kind of happy and fulfilling life we are all capable of experiencing. As a note of caution, for those who have violated children, most states demand that professionals report the incident if a specific name and place of this event is given to them. Be aware of this when doing Step Five.

Step Six: We were entirely ready to have God remove all these defects of character.

We Were Entirely Ready. As you move from Step One through Step Five, you discover a process through which you recognize powerlessness, find a God of your understanding, go inside yourself by writing an inventory and let someone else know who you really are. The very core of the program is in the first five steps. By working these steps you have learned to "trust God and clean house."

Now that you have cleaned house, you must learn how to maintain your new surroundings. It is one process to clean a dirty house, whether you got it dirty yourself or just inherited all the mess—and it is another thing entirely to make sure it never gets dirty again. That is what Step Six and the following steps are all about—preventative maintenance.

You start by being "entirely ready." This simply means that you are 100 percent ready to look at the damage that was done by all that trash, and you evaluate what you can throw away. You might be quite attached to some of that stuff. Even though it doesn't work any longer, you hesitate to give it up. Someday, some of those old behaviors might come in handy, you keep thinking. You forget that each time you try the old behavior it causes great pain. "We were entirely ready" indicates that you are finally tired of the pain. You finally realize that changing is not quite as frightening as staying the same.

To Have God. Having God in our lives is so significant for ACOSAs. Here in Step Six they are reminded that they, like everyone, are blessed by a relationship with God. They are beginning to believe that God does want the best for them, and that God wants their lives to express this new way of feeling and believing about themselves. God is willing to work with you as you continue your efforts at recovery.

Remove All. This sounds like an unrealistic, maybe even painful statement, at least from a human standpoint. "Remove" indicates loss. ACOSAs have certainly experienced loss in their lives. But to lose, or remove, all of their defects? How?

Well, it isn't up to you to decide how; it's only up to you to be ready. Remember that earlier you recognized that you don't have a

whole lot of power of your own. In Step Six you rely on God to have
the power to change you—the power you've been unable to access
in your own resources.

These Defects of Character. As you consider the term "defects
of character," you might be thinking of some of the ways you have
behaved but didn't work very well. Go ahead and get a pencil and
paper and write down what comes to mind. These aren't specific
incidents now; they are the character traits that developed from
those incidents. Reviewing your inventory should give you a good
idea of things about your character you might want changed.

For example, perhaps the way you express your anger indicates a
defect of character. Maybe the way you control, and try to manipulate, your spouse or children, or the way you pout to get your own
way, or isolate or run away from responsibility for yourself, are
things you want to change. Honesty is important in listing these
defects, because the ones you hold on to will keep you stuck in old
patterns, and you will continue to attract unhealthy people into your
life, especially in intimate relationships.

It is the experience of recovering ACOSAs that, as they become
healthier and honest themselves, they gravitate toward healthier,
honest people, and they are better able to determine who is
unhealthy. Understanding this can certainly motivate you to really
look at your defects of character and be 100 percent willing to have
God remove them. This is the real release that prevents the dust and
trash from resettling in your house.

Step Seven: We humbly asked God to remove our shortcomings.

We Humbly. Many struggle with the word "humble," having
been humiliated time and again. Humility is not the same as humiliation, although you may feel something like humiliation as you see
the devastation in your own life and the lives of those around you
caused by your defects of character. Humility, in this case, means
recognizing your true humanity. You see in Step Seven the manner
in which you should approach God. Humility means knowing that

you don't have the power to change yourself, but that God does. You come into God's presence with a humble heart, but with hope as well. And as you ask, you shall receive. As long as you don't have preconceived ideas of just how and when God will remove your defects of character, you will have them removed.

Asked God. Humility requires that we ask, not tell, God. By now you may have begun to believe that God really does want the best for you, wants you to be free of your defects of character, wants you to feel good about yourself and wants you to be attracted to healthy people. You are asking, in a sense, to do God's will.

To Remove Our Shortcomings. In Step Six you became ready. Now you push the "Go" button and ask God to take your defects of character or shortcomings. It would be nice if it happened all at once, but you will experience it as a process. In this process, God will be with you throughout your life, removing your shortcomings as you continue to identify them when they surface, as long as you are willing to ask for help.

For some ACOSAs, this step comes easily. For others, it is very hard, especially if you are holding on, still rationalizing, still defending and still gripping your defense mechanisms. In that case, Step Seven can be a painful experience. As someone once said in a meeting, "There was never anything I let go of that didn't have claw marks all over it, including my defects of character."

You can trust that if you ask, God will remove your defects of character, no matter how much you resist. If you decide to hold on to them, you will be fighting a losing battle. It is at this point that you will really need your support group. They will give you valuable feedback about any shortcomings they see you holding onto. If you aren't sure, ask questions. They will also give you support as you try new behaviors in place of the old ones that kept you so unhappy. Allow them to support you in this growth process.

Step Eight: We made a list of all persons we had harmed and became willing to make amends to them all.

We Made a List. You probably don't have any problem shopping for groceries if you've made a list. You know that the most efficient way to shop is to have a written list, instead of just mental notes, because otherwise you are likely to get home and find you have forgotten some essential items. There is a saying in Alcoholics Anonymous that you should be fearless and thorough from the very start. This is true in Step Eight. Again, take a pencil and paper in hand, and looking at your inventory, make a list of all those you have harmed. This list should include yourself as well as others, and it can also include what damage was done.

Of All Persons. Here again is that sometimes scary word: "all." It means every single one. You are, once again, being challenged to be honest. To the degree that you can be honest in making this list, you will have hope for new relationships with important people in your life.

We Had Harmed. It takes honesty to look at your life and see the people you have harmed. It is often easier to see how you have been harmed by others. In Steps Four and Five, you looked at how you have been hurt by trusted people in your life, how you have been traumatized, how you have been emotionally abandoned and how you have suffered. But if all you look at is how you have been harmed, you are only halfway healed.

Just as it can be painful for a recovering alcoholic to see how his drinking damaged those around him, so it can be painful for recovering ACOSAs to realize what they have done to hurt others. For many sex addicts, it is much more comfortable to be the victim. As a matter of fact, they have often been the victim of their own behavior, of their own past and even of recent relationships. But past victimization by others just makes it that much more difficult for these people to realize that they have actually harmed other people. The acting-out behavior is just the start of this list. The harm can be very subtle. You need to really search your mind and heart in order to complete your healing.

And Became Willing. The past tense here reminds you one more time that the hard work demanded in the previous steps is survivable. ACOSAs have worked their way through these steps before, and they have found peace and happiness on the other side. It also indicates a process. Recovery doesn't just happen overnight. Becoming willing takes time for everyone, especially if they are holding on to a victim status.

To Make Amends. What does it mean to make amends? For ACOSAs, or anyone in recovery for that matter, to make amends means acknowledging the wrong they have done and be willing to be different. You stop blaming the other person to justify your own behavior. You stop rationalizing and defending yourself. You stop avoiding responsibility. You are continuing to change in your relationships with yourself and others. You take full responsibility for what you have done, and to whom you have done it, at least on paper at this point.

To Them All. Here is that word "all" again. It seems to appear everywhere throughout the steps. By now your list should include everyone who has in any way been harmed by your actions or lack of actions. You should have found the willingness to be different with each person on that list, including yourself. No stone should be left unturned at this point, or you will still carry old guilt that will keep you stuck in your old sick patterns of thinking and relating. With names, phone numbers and accounts of damages in hand, you are ready to move on.

Step Nine: We made direct amends to such people wherever possible, except when to do so would injure them or others.

We Made Direct Amends to Such People Wherever Possible. In Step Eight, you made your list. In Step Nine, you actually go to the people on your list and make direct amends to them for your inappropriate attitudes or behaviors from the past. Notice again that this step is written in the past tense. These steps were written in the late 1930s when the first members of Alcoholics Anonymous became sober. Working these steps, especially Step Nine, was something they had to do to maintain their sobriety, so they would not have to carry the pain, shame or guilt of the past or present into their new, sober lives.

They had to be honest with themselves. And so do you as you go to each person on your list and ask for forgiveness. When you acknowledge how your behavior affected your relationships with them, you will find the most incredible freedom. Tremendous emotional weights can be lifted, and often relationships can be restored. This is not a 100 percent guarantee, since some relationships will remain fractured, but at least your side of the street will be clean.

You will begin to feel wholeness and happiness in your life, once you have made the effort to vent completely without expectations. This is a significant point. You do not make amends with the expectation that your friends or family will change their behavior. You do not make amends with the expectation that people will respond in any certain way. People may, in fact, respond when you make amends, but it is by no means the motivation for you to do what you must to get rid of what you have been carrying for so long. Inflated expectations can cause you much pain because others are not always in the same place with their recovery that you are with yours. Many people do not choose a path of recovery at all. Your personal efforts and behavior, however, can challenge them into this kind of recovery at some point in the future.

It is not a given that the other person will ask forgiveness in return, even though they may have injured you much more than you have injured them. Your goal is to clean your own slate. You are not responsible for what others leave undone, nor can their shortcomings keep you from recovering and feeling good about yourself.

Except When to Do So Would Injure Them or Others. You may become confused when you try to decide if making amends will injure the person involved, or be detrimental to other, possibly innocent people. Such confusion is best resolved with the assistance of a group, sponsor or therapist. Confusion is not to be used as an excuse not to make any amends.

What you must consider when admitting past behavior is whether or not your confession would so significantly damage the other person involved that you should not raise the issue to them. You can ask yourself, "Would this be damaging?" If you have a question, do not assume you have the answer. You could very possibly avoid making an amend that could restore a relationship, or hold on to an amend that will set you up for old behavior. Go over your list with a sponsor, support group or therapist if at all possible.

Step Ten: We continued to take personal inventory, and when we were wrong, promptly admitted it.

We Continued. Here again you must deal with the maintenance of your newly clean house. You are not letting the dust fall. You are not letting the dirt collect or the garbage overflow in the can. Here you are in a process, as in Steps Four and Five. Today, when you have been inappropriate or have violated anyone's boundaries, including your own, you don't have to wait five or ten years to make amends. You can do it as you go along.

To Take Personal Inventory. Taking a daily personal inventory is a process in which ACOSAs are able to look at each person in their life and see how they are interacting with this person. They look at their attitudes toward others and honestly evaluate them. This is not done to the point where they are unable to enjoy interactions, but it is an honest evaluation of how they respond to peers, family and in all other relationships. It also is a reminder that you inventory only your own behavior, not anyone else's.

And When We Were Wrong, Promptly Admitted It. You will be wrong. This part of Step Ten says "when," not "if" you were wrong. Many ACOSAs have been wronged, but there will still be times when you will be wrong yourself. It is important for you to stay free and not enter into a place of guilt and shame, which can push you into acting-out behavior. So in the maintenance of Step Ten, when you are wrong, you promptly admit it.

"Promptly" is significant because it keeps you from holding on to the baggage, thinking for months about whether you were or weren't wrong. Promptly means admit it right now, right here. If you have been acting inappropriately, say, "I'm sorry. Forgive me, I'm acting inappropriately." It is as simple as that. Step Ten gives you a way to stay free from the bondage of guilt and shame. It keeps you humble, which often helps you to remain healthy.

Step Eleven: We sought through prayer and meditation to improve our conscious contact with God as we understood God, praying only for knowledge of God's will for us and the power to carry that out.

We Sought Through Prayer and Meditation. This step not only tells you what you are doing, but it tells you how to do it. You are seeking. You are looking to improve your relationship with God. This step tells you to do that through prayer and meditation. Prayer is verbal, and sometimes internal, communication with God. It is such a positive experience for ACOSAs to become more aware of God in their life. This step lets you know that it is your responsibility. Seeking requires action on your part. You may have felt abandoned by God, since you put no real effort into trying to find out where he was. It has been said many times in meetings, "If you can't find God, guess who moved." You move away from God; God never moves away from you. Seeking him is all that it takes to find him.

Meditation is a deeper sense of prayer. Prayer is requesting, asking, interacting. Meditation is listening and hearing God's voice. A lot of humans experience rest and peace through meditation and are able to still the constant obsessive thinking that prevents them from hearing what God has to say: that they are significant, they are loved, and they deserve to be healthy. Meditate on God's character, on your personal relationship with him, on some scripture or recovery material you have, and allow him to really sink into your spirit. Be still, and God will speak to you.

To Improve Our Conscious Contact with God. Most ACOSAs, like many people, have an unconscious contact with God. They rely most of the time on their own thinking and resources, and they connect with God only after they have thoroughly botched their lives. Step Eleven reminds you to keep God in your conscious mind. You are then able to experience the power and love of God in a whole new way. As a result, you will experience life in a whole new way. You will have a higher sense of purpose and joy. The result of this new awareness of God on a moment-to-moment basis is a better relationship with God. As with any relationship, efforts at improving the relationship require time, energy and some sort of communication. With time you will find the method of communication that works best for you. There is no right or wrong way to do it. Just do it.

As We Understood God. It is impossible for any one of us to totally understand God. Indeed, my understanding of God might not work for you, or yours for me. The beauty of the program is that you can begin to see evidence of God in other people. Remember, this is not a job you undertake on your own. You come to a new understanding of God as you interact with the people in your support group, church or some other community of people seeking knowledge of God. As you listen, you will grow in understanding through other people's experiences of God in their lives.

Praying Only for Knowledge of God's Will for Us. By now you are beginning to see the benefits of letting go of self-will. In Step Eleven, you are gently reminded that when you pray for God's will in your life, you are asking for the absolute best solution to whatever you are facing. So often we push and push situations to turn out the way we want them to, only to find out that we got second or third or seventh or tenth best. It is a very positive thing to realize that you can trust God to have your best interests at heart. The people, places and things you have given your will over to in the past did not have your best interests at heart. You now trust God enough to say, "Not my will, but thy will be done."

And the Power to Carry That Out. You pray for knowledge of God's will, not just for the sake of having the information, but also for the power to carry it out. Having the information without the willingness or power to carry it out will not change anything. After prayer for the knowledge, you can now listen in meditation for God to tell you the things you need to do. Sometimes a path will open; sometimes God will bring to mind a defect of character that is getting in your way; and sometimes God will challenge you in the way you are behaving through intuitive thoughts or feelings. Often the power to make the changes God seems to want you to make comes from the people in your support groups. It can even come from seeing someone stuck in old behaviors. You can be motivated to change by seeing the consequences others are experiencing because of their unwillingness to act differently. Once having asked for direction and listened for guidance, you can act with assurance, knowing that if you are on the wrong track, you will come to know it. And you always know that you're not alone.

Step Twelve: Having had a spiritual awakening as the result of these steps, we tried to carry this message to others and to practice these principles in all our day-to-day living.

Having Had a Spiritual Awakening as the Result of These Steps. It is no wonder that an individual who takes the steps—and in time admits to powerlessness, admits to humanity, admits to the need for a relationship with God, actively pursues that relationship, cleans house, makes amends, and maintains this behavior—has a spiritual awakening. This spiritual awakening is the purpose of working the steps. It is an awakening in which ACOSAs discovers they have worth and value, that they are loved by God and can be loved by others, if they will only believe in their lovableness, and open up their hearts and let that love in.

This awakening to a spiritual connection with God can give ACOSAs the power to change their way of relating to themselves and the world. They can now see themselves as precious children of a loving God, and treat themselves and others accordingly.

We Tried to Carry This Message to Others. In the beginning of Alcoholics Anonymous, it was not a matter of a drunken alcoholic seeking advice and support from someone who was sober. It was the recovering alcoholic who sought out the active drinker. Bill W., the cofounder of AA, knew that if he couldn't share what he had discovered about his relationship with God and its importance to his sobriety, he wouldn't be able to stay sober. This is true for ACOSAs, too. As you progress in your recovery and become less absorbed in your own pain, you begin to recognize when others around you are in pain. You will begin to see opportunities to share your experience, strength and hope with other ACOSAs who are suffering from the same low self-esteem, dependency or independency, and lack of boundaries that you experienced. And you will share not to get them well, but to remain mindful of the miracle of recovery in your own life. Without constant reminders, you are likely to forget where your strength and health come from and become complacent.

One of the truest sayings around recovery groups is, "You can't keep it if you don't give it away." The door to recovery is opened to you because others passed this way before. It is your joy, as well as your responsibility, to keep the door open for those who follow you—and lead them to the door if they can't find it. It is the only way to ensure healing for all.

And to Practice These Principles in All Our Day-to-Day Living. Here is the most practical part of the Twelve Steps. Take what you have learned and keep doing it every day. Practice admitting your powerlessness over the problems in your life. Practice acknowledging God's ability to run your life and keep you from practicing old behaviors. Practice new thinking and behavior skills. Practice prayer and meditation. Like the athlete who must exercise daily to stay in shape, you need to practice daily the new skills you have learned, so you can stay in good emotional and spiritual shape. It took many years of practicing old behaviors for you to end up with the consequences you might be experiencing. It will take practice to become the new person you want to be. But it is possible!

Congratulations to all who embark on this journey of the Twelve Steps. These steps, when followed, are a tried and true path to healing for the ACOSA.

The Twelve Steps of Alcoholics Anonymous

1. We admitted we were powerless over alcohol—that our lives had become unmanageable.
2. We came to believe that a power greater than ourselves could restore us to sanity.
3. We made a decision to turn our will and our lives over to the care of God *as we understood him.*
4. We made a searching and fearless moral inventory of ourselves.
5. We admitted to God, to ourselves and to another human being the exact nature of our wrongs.
6. We were entirely ready to have God remove all these defects of character.
7. We humbly asked him to remove our shortcomings.
8. We made a list of all persons we had harmed and became willing to make amends to them all.
9. We made direct amends to such people wherever possible, except when to do so would injure them or others.
10. We continued to take personal inventory, and when we were wrong, promptly admitted it.
11. We sought through prayer and meditation to improve our conscious contact with God, *as we understood him,* praying only for knowledge of his will for us and the power to carry that out.
12. Having had a spiritual awakening as the result of these steps, we tried to carry this message to alcoholics and to practice these principles in all our affairs.

The Twelve-Steps of Alcoholics Anonymous Adapted for Adult Children of Sexual Addicts

1. We admitted we were powerless over our parent's sexual addiction and that our lives had become unmanageable.
2. We came to believe that a power greater than ourselves could restore us to sanity.
3. We made a decision to turn our wills and our lives over to the care of God, as we understood God.
4. We made a searching and fearless moral inventory of ourselves.
5. We admitted to God, to ourselves and to another human being the exact nature of our wrongs.
6. We were entirely ready to have God remove all these defects of character.
7. We humbly asked God to remove our shortcomings.
8. We made a list of all persons we had harmed and became willing to make amends to them all.
9. We made direct amends to such people wherever possible, except when to do so would injure them or others.
10. We continued to take personal inventory, and when we were wrong, promptly admitted it.
11. We sought through prayer and meditation to improve our conscious contact with God as we understood God, praying only for knowledge of God's will for us and the power to carry that out.
12. Having had a spiritual awakening as the result of these steps, we tried to carry this message to others and to practice these principles in all our day-to day living.

APPENDIX B

Feeling Words

Abandoned
Abused
Accepted
Accepting
Accused
Aching
Admired
Adored
Adventurous
Affectionate
Aggravated
Aggressive
Agony
Agreeable
Alienated
Alive
Alluring
Alone
Aloof
Amazed
Amused
Angry
Anguished
Annoyed
Anxious
Apart
Apathetic
Apologetic
Appreciated
Appreciative

Apprehensive
Appropriate
Approved
Argumentative
Aroused
Assertive
Astonished
Attached
Attacked
Attentive
Attractive
Aware
Awestruck
Badgered
Baited
Bashful
Battered
Beaten
Beautiful
Belittled
Belligerent
Bereaved
Betrayed
Bewildered
Blamed
Blaming
Bonded
Bored
Bothered
Brave

Breathless
Bristling
Broken-up
Bruised
Bubbly
Burdened
Burned
Callous
Calm
Capable
Captivated
Carefree
Careful
Careless
Caring
Cautious
Certain
Chased
Cheated
Cheerful
Childlike
Choked-up
Close
Cold
Comfortable
Comforted
Competent
Competitive
Complacent
Complete

Confident	Disenchanted	Frustrated
Confused	Disgusted	Full
Considerate	Disinterested	Funny
Consumed	Dispirited	Furious
Content	Distressed	Gay
Cool	Distrusted	Generous
Courageous	Distrustful	Gentle
Courteous	Disturbed	Genuine
Coy	Dominated	Giddy
Crabby	Domineering	Giving
Cranky	Doomed	Goofy
Crazy	Doubtful	Grateful
Creative	Dreadful	Greedy
Critical	Eager	Grief
Criticized	Ecstatic	Grim
Cross	Edgy	Grimy
Crushed	Edified	Grouchy
Cuddly	Elated	Grumpy
Curious	Embarrassed	Hard
Cut	Empowered	Harried
Damned	Empty	Hassled
Dangerous	Enraged	Healthy
Daring	Enraptured	Helpful
Dead	Enthusiastic	Helpless
Deceived	Enticed	Hesitant
Deceptive	Esteemed	High
Defensive	Exasperated	Hollow
Delicate	Excited	Honest
Delighted	Exhilarated	Hopeful
Demeaned	Exposed	Hopeless
Demoralized	Fake	Horrified
Dependent	Fascinated	Hostile
Depressed	Feisty	Humiliated
Deprived	Ferocious	Hurried
Deserted	Foolish	Hurt
Desirable	Forced	Hyper
Desired	Forceful	Ignorant
Despair	Forgiven	Ignored
Despondent	Forgotten	Immature
Destroyed	Free	Impatient
Different	Friendly	Important
Dirty	Frightened	Impotent

Impressed	Mystified	Ravished
Incompetent	Nasty	Ravishing
Incomplete	Nervous	Real
Independent	Nice	Refreshed
Innocent	Numb	Regretful
Insecure	Nurtured	Rejected
Insignificant	Nuts	Rejecting
Insincere	Obsessed	Rejuvenated
Inspired	Offended	Relaxed
Insulted	Open	Relieved
Interested	Ornery	Remarkable
Intimate	Out of control	Remembered
Intolerant	Overcome	Removed
Involved	Overjoyed	Repressed
Irate	Overpowered	Repulsed
Irked	Overwhelmed	Repulsive
Irrational	Pampered	Resentful
Irresponsible	Panicked	Resistant
Irritable	Paralyzed	Respected
Irritated	Paranoid	Responsible
Isolated	Patient	Responsive
Isolated	Peaceful	Restless
Jealous	Pensive	Revolved
Jittery	Perceptive	Riled
Joyous	Perturbed	Rotten
Lively	Phony	Ruined
Lonely	Pleasant	Sad
Loose	Pleased	Safe
Lost	Positive	Satiated
Loving	Powerless	Satisfied
Low	Precious	Scared
Lucky	Present	Scolded
Lustful	Pressured	Scorned
Mad	Pretty	Scrutinized
Malicious	Proud	Secure
Maudlin	Pulled apart	Seduced
Mean	Put down	Seductive
Miserable	Puzzled	Self-centered
Misunderstood	Quarrelsome	Self-conscious
Moody	Queer	Selfish
Morose	Quiet	Sensuous
Mournful	Raped	Separated

Sexy
Shattered
Shocked
Shot down
Shy
Sickened
Silly
Sincere
Sinking
Smart
Smothered
Smug
Sneaky
Snowed
Soft
Solid
Solitary
Sorry
Spacey
Special
Spiteful
Spontaneous
Squelched
Starved
Stiff
Stifled
Stimulated
Strangled
Strong
Stubborn
Stuck
Stunned
Stupid
Subdued
Submissive
Successful
Suffocated
Sure
Sweet
Sympathy
Tainted
Tearful

Tender
Tense
Terrific
Terrified
Thrilled
Ticked
Tickled
Tight
Timid
Tired
Tolerant
Tormented
Torn
Tortured
Touched
Trapped
Tremendous
Tricked
Trusted
Trustful
Trusting
Ugly
Unacceptable
Unapproachable
Unaware
Uncertain
Uncomfortable
Under control
Understanding
Understood
Undesirable
Unfriendly
Ungrateful
Unhappy
Unified
Unimpressed
Unsafe
Unstable
Unworthy
Upset
Uptight
Used

Useful
Useless
Validated
Valuable
Valued
Victorious
Violated
Violent
Voluptuous
Vulnerable
Warm
Wary
Weak
Whipped
Whole
Wicked
Wild
Willing
Wiped out
Wishful
Withdrawn
Wonderful
Worried
Worthy